The Ask

How Much is a Small Business Worth?

Published by 3Fi Media Ltd.
Richmond, BC, Canada

Liisa Atva, author
The Ask: How Much is a Small Business Worth?

ISBN 978-1-7750035-0-2

Editors: Susan Chilton and Bernard Simon
Cover and interior design: Toni Serofin
Author photo: Sandra Steier
Illustrator of the three entrepreneurs: Barry Collins

Printed and bound by Printorium in Canada
First Printing December 2017

For bulk book purchases or speaking engagements contact the author at liisaa@telus.net.

www.liisaatva.com

This book is dedicated to small business owners

— my kind of hero —

and the true backbone of the Canadian economy.

Contents

About the Author

Liisa Atva is a Chartered Professional Accountant (CPA) and a Chartered Business Valuator with over 30 years of experience auditing, analyzing and advising businesses of all sizes. When she was a teenager it was a family friend, the respected owner of an auto body shop in a small town, who first sparked her interest in a business career. It was possible to have your very own business, she marvelled. After articling as a CPA, she specialized in business valuations, before joining a startup investment bank that she helped grow to 90 employees and $13 billion in transactions. In 2008, she returned to her roots — small business — to focus on writing, teaching, and mentoring current and future business owners.

1

Let's Get Started

So you're thinking of selling your business. Or perhaps you're bringing in a partner or investor to take it to the next level. Maybe you are the potential buyer or investor. Whatever the case, I'm guessing the first question that popped into your head was: How much is the business worth? In other words, if you're a seller: How much will I get? Or, if you're a buyer or investor: How much should I pay?

Coming up with the right amount can make the difference between closing a deal or not closing one. If the seller overvalues the business, potential buyers or investors may be scared off. On the reality TV show *Dragon's Den*, entrepreneurs pitch their businesses to the "Dragons," a panel of successful and experienced investors. If you've watched the show you likely will have heard the Dragons' all-too-frequent lament: "You've got the value wrong."

Even worse, if the seller undervalues the business, he or she will end up giving away part of what they worked so hard to create. As for buyers, if they overpay, they run the risk of being short of funds to run or grow the business, or find that they're unable to sell it for a profit in the future.

This book should help lead you in the right direction. Don't worry if you're not familiar with accounting, finance, or business terms. I've tried to explain things in a way that a typical small business owner — one without a business degree — can easily understand. At the end of the book, you'll also find a list of the key words and terms used.

With that in mind, we'll navigate the process of valuing a business through the eyes of Mike, Joe and Elle, three entrepreneurs who have tough decisions to make about their futures and the businesses they are involved in. Though the characters and their stories are fictional, they are, as they say in the movies, "inspired by true events."

Before we introduce Joe, Mike and Elle, you should know what this book covers — and what it doesn't.

Our focus throughout is on small businesses. There is no universal definition of a small business. Industry Canada defines it by number of employees: fewer than 50 for a business in the service sector, or fewer than 100 for a firm that produces goods. Statistics Canada normally considers a firm with fewer than 50 full-time employees a small business, though some of its publications use a cut-off point of $2 million in annual sales. The Canadian Federation of Independent Business, a lobbying group representing owners of small and mid-sized enterprises, does not have a size limit for membership, but its members must be privately owned companies that are not publicly traded.

Much of the information in this book also applies to valuing larger enterprises, because the basic concepts and principles are the same. But scale introduces complexities: some issues that are relevant only to valuing larger companies are not covered here. As well, owners of mid-sized and larger companies are often well served by professional advisers who can help determine what the business is worth. If you are the owner of a small business, or aspire to be, you can also hire experts, and that can often be a smart move (more on that later). This book is aimed at those who want to understand what their business is worth and why, whether they ultimately value it themselves or not.

The most important thing you need to know when selling, buying, or investing in a business is how much it's really worth.

Owning a business has many benefits, but not all of them can be measured in dollars and cents. For example, some owners see great value in controlling their own destiny, others in helping family members by giving them jobs. Still others see a small business as a way of turning a passion into a career, working with people they like and trust, or giving themselves status in their community.

These benefits undoubtedly have value, but that value is often in the eye of the beholder, whether buyer or seller, and thus difficult to quantify. Often based on subjective opinion and experience, rather than concrete data, these benefits may have little value to anyone other than a specific individual, and thus may be irrelevant to other parties involved in buying, selling or investing in the business.

Throughout this book, "worth" and "value" are used interchangeably but, in all cases, they refer only to dollar amounts. As we will see, Joe, Mike and Elle's questions — "How much can I get for my company?" "How much will I have to pay?" "How much of my business will I have to give up?" — are thus about the money or dollar value of their businesses.

You may have come across the term business "evaluation." Although not wrong, the word "evaluation" can be broader in scope than the dollar value. It also means judging the merit of something. Does the business have growth potential? Is it well managed? Valuation (without the "e") is a more specific term, commonly used in the context of determining what a business is worth in dollar terms. You may also have heard the phrase "business appraisal." It is often used in the US, but less so in Canada.

To recap: valuing a business is the process of determining the dollar value of that business; a business valuation is the result of that process.

Which brings us back to our central question: What is the value of a business? The short answer is: the price that someone is willing to pay for it. But that doesn't tell the whole story. Until a business is actually sold, it's impossible to know with any certainty what someone would be willing to pay. As we'll see later, the timing of a sale and the parties' negotiating ability, among other hard-to-measure factors, may also affect the price.

You should also know that valuing a business is as much an art as a science. It is seldom — if ever — possible to simply plug numbers into a formula. That said, although the process of determining what a business is worth may seem a daunting task, it need not be, particularly for smaller businesses.

My goal is not to turn you, the reader, into an expert in business valuation. Rather, I hope to give you a basic grasp of the key issues and concepts. You'll get a better idea what's involved in valuing a business as we delve into the stories of our three entrepreneurs.

2

Joe, Mike and Elle: A Tale of Three Entrepreneurs

Joe

Joe glanced up from the obituary section of the newspaper and called out to his wife, "Sixty! Not much older than me!"

Frank Kay, Joe's former boss, had died suddenly from a heart attack.

"Maybe it's time to retire," a shaken Joe mused.

His wife nodded approvingly. “That’s a good idea. We would have more time for travel, golf, and the grandchildren.”

“Hmm. Maybe I should sell my business. I wonder how much it’s worth?”

Joe, an electronics engineer, started Niche Power 25 years ago. Before that, he held engineering and management roles at a number of other companies. The last time he worked for someone else was a stint as the sales and marketing manager of Cable Tech, a supplier of backup power equipment to the cable TV industry. During his four years there, Joe helped expand sales from $1 million to $10 million a year.

While at Cable Tech, Joe saw an opportunity to develop a new product line and presented the idea to his boss, Frank, the owner. But Frank wasn’t comfortable taking Cable Tech in that direction, and he insisted that Joe stick to selling existing products. Frustrated, Joe quit.

“I should start my own business and be my own boss,” he said to himself.

Joe tossed around the idea of developing the new product with three people he’d worked with at other companies: a design engineer, a software developer and an accountant. They all agreed that the idea had merit, so incorporated a company they called Niche Power. Joe held 40 percent of the shares, and each of the others 20 percent. The three put up $1,000 each and Joe agreed to fund the rest of the development costs.

They built a prototype but, a year later, Niche Power still had no sales and Joe’s three partners were reluctant to commit more money or time to the venture. Joe offered to buy back their shares for the $1,000 each had invested. The engineer and software developer accepted the offer. The accountant, however, wouldn’t accept less than $6,000. “The company doesn't have much value now, but it might have in the future," he argued. Eager to be done with the accountant and reluctant to spend money fighting him, Joe forked out the $6,000.

Joe soldiered on alone. One potentially large sale fell through. Discouraged, but not ready to give up, Joe attended a trade fair. There, he came across a Japanese-made product that he thought he might be able to sell in North America. He obtained the Canadian distribution rights and, finally, two years after starting Niche Power, Joe had his first sale. He went on to negotiate distribution rights for other suppliers' products, and to develop new products of his own. By the time Joe was considering selling Niche Power, it had grown to $1.5 million in annual sales, with five full-time employees and a 2,000-square-foot office and warehouse in an industrial area near Toronto.

Joe is not the only one nearing retirement and thinking of selling his business. According to Statistics Canada, 47 percent of small business owners in Canada are older than 50. If they are not already contemplating retirement, most soon will be. Indeed, a CIBC research report by Benjamin Tal back in 2012 found that half of Canadian business owners planned to exit or transfer ownership of their businesses within 10 years. With just over one million businesses in Canada, that means more than half a million businesses, the vast majority of them small enterprises, are set to change hands over the next decade or so.

Selling a business, even a small one, is a complex process that requires numerous steps. Among them: determining what the business is worth; marketing it to potential buyers; negotiating the details; and preparing legal agreements to close the sale. The first step — determining what the business is worth — is crucial. If the seller and potential buyer can't agree on a price, a sale will not take place. And yet many business owners have little or no idea how to arrive at that price.

Valuing a business draws on a broad spectrum of disciplines including economics, finance, accounting, tax, and law — all mixed in with good old common sense. Most small business owners — 62 percent, according to Statistics Canada — do not have a university degree and, even if they do, it may not be in one of those disciplines. However, as many successful business owners have shown, you don't need a degree to run a business. Nor should you need a degree to value one.

Joe started his business from scratch and ran it successfully for 25 years. But when it came to valuing it, he realized that he was out of his depth. He turned to his accountant Dan, a Chartered Professional Accountant (CPA) and a partner in Dunfell & Steveston, a small, local accounting firm. Dan's expertise is accounting and income tax. He completed a business degree prior to becoming a CPA, so is very knowledgeable about finance and economics. During his 20 years with Dunfell & Steveston, Dan has also gained a working knowledge of the legal issues that small businesses typically encounter. He seems to have all the bases covered but, to Joe's surprise, Dan readily admits that he is not an expert in business valuations. However, Dan offers to introduce Joe to someone who is. I'll describe the various types of business valuation experts in *Chapter 17 — Hiring an Expert.*

Understanding some or all of the subjects listed above may give you the building blocks to value a business. However, the blocks in themselves are not enough; you also need to know how to put them together. Where do you learn how to value businesses? Typically even business schools do not teach business valuation, other than perhaps on a limited basis at the post-graduate level. For self-learners, there are some excellent textbooks, including some Canadian ones.[1] But most of these are not an easy read, and appear to be more geared towards someone with a solid foundation in business seeking to become a valuation expert.

Since valuing a business is an essential part of the buying or selling process, why is more information not available on how to do it? Perhaps there has not been enough demand or "need to know." Businesses do not typically change hands often; owners may buy or sell one just once in a lifetime. However, given the number of businesses that could change hands over the next decade, many more people will need to know. Like Joe, the vast majority of owners — 76 percent according to Statistics Canada — start their businesses from scratch. Like Joe, most face the prospect of selling their business without ever having bought one. As a result, the first time that they need to figure out how much their business is worth is when they are preparing to sell it.

Mike

We've met Joe, who is looking to sell his business. Now let's introduce Mike, who is eager to buy one. Mike, who is 40, moved to Vancouver from China five years ago. Despite having 15 years of experience as a medical lab technician, he was unable to find a position in his field. For the past four years, he has worked for Blind Ninja, a window-blind installation company serving primarily commercial clients. With a small inheritance he received recently, Mike is now thinking of buying his own blind-installation business.

---

1 Johnson, Howard E., *Business Valuation*, Chartered Professional Accountants of Canada, 2012

Luckily, Home Décor Blinds, a US-based franchisor, is looking to set up in Canada and has been actively marketing franchises across the country. Mike does not have experience running a business so the idea of a big company providing training, marketing support, advertising, and business leads is appealing. In return, Home Décor charges a $15,000 one-time franchise-licensing fee, a territory fee of $10,000 for a designated area of Vancouver, and a royalty of four percent on annual sales. Home Décor makes no claims on potential revenue for the territory it is offering Mike, but it does disclose the average sales of its American franchisees. Mike would, of course, have to buy his blinds from Home Décor. Mike estimates the total upfront costs of becoming a Home Décor Blinds franchisee at $75,000, including buying a van and tools, and paying for his first order of blinds.

But Mike then discovers another option. He could buy blinds made in China at a much lower cost than available locally. Blind Ninja, Mike's employer, does not currently sell blinds; it just installs those that its customers provide. Mike sees an opportunity for Blind Ninja to also sell the blinds that it installs. When Mike mentions this to his boss Bill, the owner of Blind Ninja, Bill confides that he would like to expand his business to Alberta, but needs capital to do so. Bill offers to make Mike an equal partner and sell him 50 percent of Blind Ninja for $30,000.

Mike weighs the two options: purchasing a Home Décor franchise or buying into Blind Ninja. He decides to go with Blind Ninja. His main reason is the lower upfront investment of $30,000, which is less than half the cost of the Home Décor franchise option. Also, Blind Ninja is well established in the area with revenues for the prior year of $170,000, and has the potential to become a supplier of blinds, opening a new window of opportunity. As well, Mike likes the idea of having a partner, especially someone he already knows and works well with. Still, he wonders, "Is $30,000 a reasonable price to pay for 50 percent of Blind Ninja?"

Elle

Unlike Joe and Mike, Elle is not looking to buy or sell a business. Rather, she is seeking an outside investor for her venture.

After graduating from high school, Elle supported herself playing online poker on various US-based sites. After the US Justice Department shut down the most popular poker sites and started seizing bank accounts, Elle decided to further her studies at Simon Fraser University's Beedie School of Business. With her interest in poker, which involves assessing probabilities, she especially looked forward to her statistics classes. But Elle noticed that many of her classmates were not enjoying the lectures as much as she was. Reflecting back on how much fun she had when she first learned to play poker — especially when she started winning — she figured there must be a more interesting way to learn about statistics.

Reasoning that learning is more fun when it's a game, she wondered if she couldn't find a way of adapting her love of poker to the world of statistics. Through poker, she had learned about probability, strategy, risk and reward, and patience — useful skills, she realized, not only for understanding statistics but also for investing. And so Elle came up with the idea for *Poker Head*, a video game that introduces statistics while playing her favourite game.

Elle approached her friend Cole, a freelance video artist familiar with the gaming world. "How much would it cost to develop the game?" she asked.

Cole explained: "First you should make a demo — it's like a pilot or proof of concept. You can use that to gauge interest. That takes a minimum of three months and costs around $30,000 for artwork and coding. If that goes well, you're looking at another $50,000 to $100,000 to get to the functioning game stage, and that takes at least a year or two."

"Then you're done?" Elle asked hopefully.

"Not yet. Two-thirds of a game's cost is in the marketing. And that could be another $250,000. But then you have more funding options. You can either release it under early access, or find a distributor. With early access, the game doesn't have to be perfect or complete, but it needs to be playable. You get full price for it and give buyers updates as you go along.

The buyers give you feedback and basically stress-test the game. I heard that a local game developer made $2 or $3 million on early access with one of his games. Or you could sell it to a distributor. They'll pay for the rest of the development and the marketing, but they'll take 80 percent."

"I only have $25,000. Would you do the demo for that?"

"That, plus a 10 percent interest in the game," Cole countered.

Realizing the value of Cole's expertise, Elle agreed to his terms. Cole did the artwork and hired another freelancer to write the code. Sure enough, after three months of 16-hour days, they had a demo. They posted it on several gaming-community sites and soon garnered 10,000 views and many positive comments — a rare achievement, according to Cole.

"The internet is full of really bored teenagers who rip everything to shreds," he observed.

Now, they needed the $50,000 to $100,000 to take the demo to the functioning game stage. But Elle was out of money, and neither she nor Cole knew any potential investors. They posted a note on Reddit Business: "Developing a video game. Fantastic art. At demo stage. Positive feedback. No money. No connections. Need an investor." A response came in the very next day: "If your idea is good, I have money." After exchanging a few emails, the investor suggested they meet.

But Elle was worried. "How much of the business will we have to give him?" she wondered.

Joe, Mike and Elle come from very different backgrounds. Joe has run a successful business for 25 years without a business degree or formal business training. Mike, a lab technician, has a diploma from a technical college in China. His business education consists of an eight-week course on starting your own business offered one night a week at a local college. Elle is working on her university degree. Having supported herself since high school by playing poker, she has no practical work experience at all.

What Joe, Mike and Elle have in common, however, is an entrepreneurial spirit, a hunger to be their own boss, and the self-confidence to take a risk. They are unfazed by their lack of relevant experience, acumen, or education. None of them has ever bought or sold a business before.

Yet, as we noted earlier, you need to have an idea of a business's value before you can even begin the process of buying or selling one. In Joe's case, he needs to know how much to ask for his business. If he overvalues it, he may scare away potential purchasers. If he undervalues it, he may not sell it for as much as he could. In each case, the cost of getting the value wrong could be high.

An experienced business valuator I know was hired to advise whether an asking price of $500,000 was reasonable for a business that his client was considering buying. After his review, the valuator concluded that the business was worth no more than $250,000. The seller's broker agreed that the asking price was likely too high, but the seller had insisted that he would settle for no less. The valuator's client offered a compromise, but the broker refused even to present it to the seller. "He wouldn't even let us get in the same room as the seller," said the valuator. A year later, the business had still not sold. Ultimately, it went bankrupt.

Mike has already been presented with an asking price for Blind Ninja.

He now needs to determine if the asking price reflects the value of the business. Price and value are not necessarily the same. As Warren Buffett puts it: "Price is what you pay. Value is what you get." If Mike agrees to the asking price, does that mean the value of the business has been determined? Maybe yes, maybe no. The parties' negotiating abilities are also part of the equation. Bill may have asked more for the business than he thought it was really worth, expecting to have the price negotiated down. If Mike is either unable or unwilling to negotiate a lower price, he may well end up paying more than he needed to.

Elle is in the same situation as Joe. She needs to value her business and she faces the same risk: if she asks too much, she could drive investors away; if she asks too little, she will end up giving up a larger percentage of the business than she need have, an unnecessary sacrifice.

It is often difficult for owners to separate themselves from their businesses, and look at their enterprises unemotionally. How much money or effort an owner has invested in a business may sometimes have little bearing on its value. As one of the Dragons once said, "We don't pay for past mistakes."

The same can be said for opportunity cost, which is the value of what you have given up to achieve something else. If Elle could have made $20,000 playing poker during the three months that she was working on Poker Head that does not mean that it is worth at least $20,000. Indeed, Poker Head could be worth very little if there is no market for the game.

Likewise, however much money Joe thinks he needs for retirement has no relevance at all to the value of his business. Let's assume that he takes a salary of $80,000 a year. He would like to sell the company and invest the proceeds in a low-risk investment that would continue to pay him the same amount. Is that a reasonable expectation? Assuming an annual return of four percent, it would take an investment of $2 million to generate that $80,000. However, a business that requires time and effort is quite different from a passive investment; it has more inherent risk, and potentially a higher return. As we'll see later, perceived risk and reward have an impact on value. Needless to say, prospective buyers of Joe's business don't care how much money he thinks he needs to retire.

Now, let's turn to the issues that Joe, Mike and Elle will have to grapple with as they work out how much their businesses are worth.

3

Market Method: Good in Theory, but...

If the value of a business isn't based on how much money, time or effort someone has put into it, or on how much a seller thinks he or she needs, how do we determine what it's worth? A business is essentially an investment. If we look at how other types of significant investments are valued, perhaps we can apply similar concepts to business valuation.

An investment in residential real estate is one that small business owners will be familiar with. Let's look at an example. A house or condo is typically valued using a "market method." With the help of a real estate agent or real estate's Multiple Listing Service (MLS), we estimate its value by using "comparables"; in other words, recent sales of similar properties in the same neighbourhood. One home is never exactly the same as another. However, unless the property is one-of-a-kind — say, the only 10,000-square-foot mansion on a private beach — it is usually possible to find reasonably comparable transactions. Can we value a business by finding out what a comparable one sold for?

According to Statistics Canada's 2011 National Household Survey, there are about nine million dwellings in Canada. Therefore, the likelihood of finding a comparable property is relatively high. On the other hand, there are only one million businesses in Canada. That may sound like a lot, but it is just one-ninth the number of dwellings, significantly shrinking the potential number of comparables. As well, while Statistics Canada classifies dwellings into ten types, such as single-detached house, semi-detached house, row house, apartment, etc., it recognizes 918 different industries (2017 North American Industry Classification System). That's right: 918, from potato farming to aerospace parts manufacturing. To make comparisons even more difficult, two seemingly similar businesses, such as two restaurants on the same street, may have little in common — one may be upscale, popular and profitable, the other could be a dive.

Even if you can find a comparable business, another problem with using this market method is lack of information. While you can usually find out how much a house sold for, the same does not apply to businesses. Most small businesses are private companies or proprietorships; they are not required to disclose change-of-ownership and sales information to the public and, as a result, very few do.

Small businesses are so unique that valuing one based on the sale of a comparable business is rarely possible.

Information on publicly held companies, on the other hand, is often available. So why not use prices at which public company shares trade on the stock exchange as a comparable? That is also easier said than done. Even if a small business and a public company are in the same industry, they will seldom be comparable. Elle's business, Poker Head, and the NASDAQ-listed company Electronic Arts are both game developers. Electronic Arts reported revenues of US$4.4 billion in 2016. If Poker Head managed to pull in even $1 million in a year that would be quite an accomplishment. Electronic Arts has a huge portfolio of popular games and over 200 million registered players; Poker Head owns just one game.

There are smaller publicly listed gaming companies, but they are still much larger than Poker Head. A company typically needs to reach a certain size before it can go public. For example, to list on the TSX Venture Exchange's Tier Two, the lowest thresholds are for companies in the industrial, technology or life-sciences sector. Even they must have at least $750,000 of net tangible assets or annual revenues of $500,000, which is significantly larger than many small businesses.

Additionally, the number of shares of a publicly listed company that trade on any given day is typically only a small fraction of the total number of its outstanding shares. Electronic Arts, for example, had over 300 million outstanding shares in May 2017. The 50-day average daily volume of shares traded was almost three million — one percent of the outstanding shares. The trading price for a small percentage of the outstanding number of shares does not necessarily reflect the value of a larger block of shares, or of the company as a whole. While there might be many buyers for small blocks of shares, there may be considerably fewer for a larger one. In order to sell a larger block of shares, the price might have to drop considerably. (An exception to this might be a takeover offer, when the bidder may offer a premium to the trading price.)

The shares of publicly listed companies also have higher liquidity, which means they can be readily bought or sold through a stock exchange, often within a few seconds. The shares of private companies are not nearly as liquid, and the process of finding a buyer is far more difficult and time-consuming. The combination of higher liquidity for public company shares, and the relatively small fraction of the outstanding shares being sold, typically results in a greater number of potential buyers and, therefore, higher prices for shares of publicly listed companies as compared to small private ones.

Another complication is that a valuation applies at a specific point in time. Even if one could find a comparable business, circumstances may have changed dramatically since it was sold. When valuing a small business, there will likely be few, if any, instances of a comparable sale to make the market method feasible. With that in mind, we need to consider other valuation methods.

4

Rules of Thumb: Simple But Often Misleading

As explained in *Chapter 3*, the difficulty of finding a "comparable sale" usually rules out the market method for valuing a business. Even so, businesses in the same industry do share some common features. Can these commonalities perhaps be used in some way to value a business? "Rule of thumb" valuation methods try to do this. According to Wikipedia, "A rule of thumb is a principle with broad application that is not intended to be strictly accurate or reliable for every situation. It is an easily learned and easily applied procedure for approximately calculating or recalling some value, or for making some determination."

As an example of a rule of thumb, let's use the 19th century adage that your child's final adult height will be double that on his or her second birthday. When my son was two, I pulled out a tape measure — he was exactly three feet tall. By the time he'd stopped growing, he had indeed reached six feet. Even though the rule of thumb held, I took it as a coincidence. If I'd polled my friends with children, I'm sure I would have found many cases where it did not hold. Rules of thumb for valuing businesses are no different; they are easily applied, but not necessarily accurate or reliable.

When I mentioned to a teacher friend that I was writing a book about valuing businesses, his response was: "That's easy! Isn't it just three times gross profit (total revenue minus the cost of goods sold)?" He was only half joking. Although he had not personally been involved in buying or selling a business, and couldn't recall where he'd heard that, he thought it was common knowledge. According to one business broker, "at the moment, most smaller companies are selling for three to five times EBITDA." (EBITDA is an acronym for earnings before interest, income tax, depreciation and amortization and is explained further in *Chapter 7*.) "Typically a firm trades for five to six times earnings," said another. "A business might typically sell for 'two times sales' or 'one times sales,'" according to a different broker.

Most rules of thumb are based on some multiple of revenue, sales, or earnings. Which one should you use? Do they apply to every size of business in every industry? There are several US-based online and/or print publications that offer rules of thumb for specific sectors. These include The Business Reference Guide (BRG), Pratt's Stats, and BIZCOMPS. BRG lists over 700 types of business, including small retailers, auto repair shops, bars, beauty shops, bed and breakfasts, daycares, drug stores, dry-cleaners, fast-food franchises, grocery stores, laundries, restaurants, retail shops, travel and insurance agencies, and accounting, dental and medical practices...the list goes on.

These publications compile their rules of thumb based on actual sales of primarily small, privately held, owner-operated businesses, as reported in surveys of business brokers, consultants and accountants. As with any information provided voluntarily, there is no guarantee that it is either complete or accurate. For businesses in the sectors listed, a rule of thumb can provide a rough estimate of value. But all the publications include cautionary disclaimers and suggest a careful consideration of other appropriate methods. According to BRG, "The information in this book presents a 'ballpark' for putting a price on a business. The marketplace determines the ultimate price."

The rules of thumb contained in these guides are typically based on a percentage of revenue or earnings, with or without adjustments for various expenses. For example, the rule of thumb for fast-food chains is 35 to 45 percent of annual sales plus inventory and equipment. Using this formula, a fast-food restaurant with annual sales of $100,000 would have a value of $35,000 to $45,000 plus inventory and equipment.

BRG makes a bold assertion: "We have found over the years that the rules of thumb come just about as close to what a business is worth as any other pricing method." I would take that with a grain of salt, given that BRG is selling a service based on the rules of thumb in its own publications. Furthermore, unless you apply other methods, how would you know how close the rule of thumb comes to the value of your own business?

Valuing a business is more of an art than a science, hence there is no "formula."

There are other potential problems with using these rules of thumb. First, the publications are based on US data that may or may not apply to Canada. Second, they often ignore profitability. If two businesses have the same revenue but one is profitable and the other not, they are unlikely to have the same value. Even if two businesses in the same industry report the same revenues and profits, other factors could make one worth significantly more than the other. One may be in a neighbourhood with a growing population, the other in a town that is dying. Third, not every type of business is included. According to BRG: "Keep in mind that if it's not in the guide, we don't really have a rule of thumb for that business."

Even so, rules of thumb are sometimes useful. They often play an important role in valuing professional practices, such as those of accountants, financial advisers, and insurance brokers. Often with these practices, what is being sold is a "book of business" or a client list, rather than a company. Buyers are typically only interested in the revenue that the client list can generate, and not the rest of the business, which includes employees, premises, office furniture, equipment or other assets. Buyers of professional practices may already have their own established business, and are looking just to add a roster of new clients. When you strip a client list from the rest of a business, it becomes more easily comparable, making rules of thumb more relevant. Each type of professional practice typically has its own rules of thumb, and these are not difficult to find.

A rule of thumb may be useful as a rough estimate of value, or to double-check a value determined by other methods, such as those in the chapters to come. Because using a rule of thumb to determine value is typically an easy and inexpensive exercise, there is no harm in doing so, as long as other valuation methods are also used.

Despite their limitations, rules of thumb are often used to value small businesses. Buyers and sellers of small businesses are typically not experienced business valuators and rules of thumb have the distinct appeal of being easy to use. Using a different valuation method, even if it is a more appropriate one, could be like joining a game in progress and then asking to play by a different set of rules: you might find yourself thrown out of the game if you aren't willing to play by the rules others want to use. And that may not be a bad thing if it saves you from buying a business that is overvalued.

An industry in which rules of thumb are often used is restaurants. Coincidently, in Canada businesses in the accommodation and food service sector go bankrupt at four times the average rate of all businesses. Paying more for a business than it's worth increases the possibility of a negative outcome. You'll do far better by using more sophisticated methods to find businesses that may be undervalued by owners relying solely on rules of thumb. You can then scoop them up at a bargain price.

5

There Must Be a Better Way

If rules of thumb are not the best way to value a business, what is? To find the answer, let's continue with thinking of a business as an investment. We buy investments expecting a financial return. We put money into savings accounts expecting to earn interest. We buy stocks expecting to earn dividends or ultimately to sell them for more than we paid. The price an investor is willing to pay for an investment depends on how much cash he or she expects to receive from it, and when.

Cash flows from investments that pay a fixed interest rate, such as term deposits (also called guaranteed investment certificates or GICs) can easily be predicted by multiplying the amount deposited by the interest rate for the term selected. For example, a $20,000 one-year term deposit that pays interest of two percent a year will generate $400 in interest.

Let's consider an investment higher on the complexity scale than a term deposit. If you were considering buying a house to rent out, a thorough understanding of the following would help you forecast the expected cash flow from the house.

1. ***The neighbourhood.*** The potential resale value of the house will be impacted by neighbourhood amenities such as schools, shopping, community centres and access to transit. Crime rates, potential zoning changes and development plans should also be considered.

2. ***The house itself.*** Determine the potential rental income, property taxes, and the cost of maintenance, repairs, and desired renovations.

3. ***Economic outlook.*** Understand the potential impact of vacancy rates, mortgage interest rates, and projected changes in property values.

You need to have similar information about a potential business investment. Although, instead of learning about a neighbourhood, you're learning about an industry — though the neighbourhood may also be important if it's a business for which location matters. Instead of learning about a house, you're learning about a business. Instead of learning about the economic outlook for rentals, you're learning about the economic outlook for that sector and businesses in general. Bear in mind, however, that sizing up even the simplest small business is typically far more complicated than scoping out a rental house.

We'll look at each of these factors in more depth during "due diligence." The term conveys a certain seriousness that is captured in the Investopedia definition: "Generally due diligence refers to the care a reasonable person should take before entering into an agreement or transaction with another party." Due diligence can also be described as "appropriate attentiveness" or "expected thoroughness."

The industry

There is no one-size-fits-all process to conduct due diligence, but starting with information about the industry can provide a yardstick against which a specific business can be measured. To learn about the industry, researching online and through other sources is a good start, but it's even more important to get the perspective of people close to the business and the industry it operates in. Talk to its owners, managers, competitors, industry groups and anyone else you can find who knows more about the industry and business than you do. Consider the questions below.

1. ***What sector is it in?*** This is not always self-evident because a business can have several facets to its operations. A useful guide is the North American Industry Classification System (NAICS). Niche Power, for example, would fall under more than one category: NAICS #335311 — power, distribution and speciality transformers manufacturing, and #417230 — industrial machinery, equipment and supplies merchant wholesaler. Poker Head would fall under #541515 — video game design and development, and Blind Ninja under #561799 — other services to buildings and dwellings. Understanding what sector the business is in will help you make comparisons with other companies, when such information is available, and enhance your awareness of factors that may affect the industry as a whole.

2. ***What is the outlook and growth potential for the industry?*** For example, the outlook for video stores dimmed as the popularity of Netflix and other on-demand services grew. By contrast, the growth potential of businesses that cater to seniors should improve as Canadians live longer.

3. ***Are there developments in the industry that will have an impact on the business?*** These can include changes to taxes, legislation, technology, climate change, or competitors entering the field. For example, the so-called "sharing economy" is having a big impact on hotels through Airbnb, and on taxis through Uber.

4. ***Are there barriers to entering the industry?*** Barriers can be financial, regulatory, competitive, or anything else that makes it difficult for a new business to break into the field. For example, the City of Vancouver tightly controls the number of taxi licences, making it difficult and costly for newcomers to obtain one.

The business

An in-depth review of the business itself is, without a doubt, the most crucial — and most challenging — aspect of due diligence. You will need to find out the following:

1. ***Background information.*** Who owns the business? What is its history? Where is it located?

2. ***Products and services.*** What does the business do? What products or services does it provide and what makes these unique? Does it have proprietary technology or knowledge?

3. ***Sales and marketing.*** How does the business market and sell its products or services? Who are its customers? Is it dependent on a small number of them? Has the business recently gained or lost key customers? Does it have a competitive advantage? What is the growth potential?

4. ***Reputation.*** What is the reputation of the business in its sector, and how does it compare to its competitors?

5. ***Production.*** How does it produce what it sells? Does it have manufacturing operations? How does it distribute its products? Is it dependent on any suppliers for key materials or components?

6. ***Management and employees.*** What role does the owner play in the business? Can it operate without him or her? Is there a management team? Is the business able to attract and retain qualified employees?

I have saved the most important question for last. In fact, it's so important it requires its own section:

7. ***What do the financial statements show?*** By the time you've learned about the industry and the business by asking the above questions, the financial statements will be that much more relevant and revealing.

Financial statements

Businesses that are incorporated — set up as companies and thus as separate legal entities from the owner — are required by law to prepare financial statements. These may be prepared according to Generally Accepted Accounting Principles (GAAP), a common set of accounting principles, standards and procedures, or to a lesser standard if the financial statements are compiled for tax purposes only. Canadian GAAP includes International Financial Reporting Standards (IFRS) and Accounting Standards for Private Enterprises (ASPE), a simpler alternative for private enterprises only. Given the cost, a company will generally prepare GAAP financial statements only if required to, or requested to by current or potential investors and lenders.

Financial statements compiled for tax purposes are typically much simpler. At a minimum, they must include an income statement, which includes the business's sales, revenue and expenses, and a balance sheet, which lists the business's assets — in other words, the things that it owns — and its liabilities — the amounts that it owes to others. Financial statements prepared by the company itself are acceptable for tax purposes; the Canada Revenue

Agency (CRA) does not require them to be reviewed by an external auditor or accountant.

Can you rely on a business's financial statements to be complete and accurate? Financial statements prepared according to GAAP and audited by a Chartered Professional Accountant (CPA) have the highest level of assurance. Note, however, that assurance is not the same as a guarantee; although it is rare, auditors can be misled. Most small businesses do not have their financial statements audited; it is often an expense that is not justified. Financial statements that have been reviewed but not audited by a CPA, provide less assurance than audited ones, but are usually adequate for our purposes.

CPAs may also compile financial statements based on information provided by the business. For these the CPA gives no assurance other than that the statements are arithmetically correct and not false or misleading — in the opinion of the business, not the CPA. The degree to which you can rely on compiled financial statements depends on your comfort level with the information provided by the business to the CPA. Generally, the involvement of a CPA should provide more comfort than financial statements prepared solely by the business with no outside involvement.

If a business is not incorporated as a company and operates as a proprietorship or partnership, its income is included on the proprietor or partner's personal tax return. A business operated as such is not required to prepare separate financial statements. Instead, for tax purposes the CRA requires a "statement of business or professional activities" in a prescribed format similar to an income statement. There is also no requirement to prepare a balance sheet.

At minimum, you should ask to see either the company's financial statements or, for proprietorships and partnerships, a statement of business or professional activities. If the owner can't or won't produce them, you may have cause for concern. Unless the business has not yet completed its first year, a lack of financial statements or statement of business activities could be a sign that the business, proprietor or partnership has not filed its tax returns. If financial information is available but the owner is reluctant to provide it, that should also be a red flag. A few years ago, a friend was looking to buy a florist business. The owner wanted the buyer to take over the lease and pay an amount equal to three years' sales, yet he refused to provide any financial statements. "Believe me, it's a good location, good sales," he insisted. Needless to say, my friend walked away.

As an incorporated company, Niche Power prepares annual financial statements for tax purposes. One of the conditions of an outstanding bank loan is that a firm of CPAs must review the statements each year, though there is no requirement that they be audited. Niche Power's annual financial statements are reviewed by Dunfell & Steveston. Niche Power also prepares monthly financial statements and a five-year forecast of net income, neither of which are reviewed by the CPAs.

Blind Ninja operates as a proprietorship. Bill, the owner, prepares the required statement of business activities every year himself. He does not prepare monthly statements or a forecast.

Poker Head is less than a year old. Elle keeps a list of expenses incurred but has not yet prepared any formal financial statements. However, she has prepared a five-year cash flow forecast, including revenue and expenses, to show potential investors.

Income statements and statements of business or professional activities provide similar information. I will refer to all of these as income statements. When conducting due diligence, you will want to look at income statements for the past few years and for the latest interim period available. Proprietorships often prepare income statements only at the business year-end. But business conditions and thus a company's financial health can change quickly, even in the space of a few months. If several months have elapsed since year-end, a potential buyer should ask the seller to prepare a more recent income statement. However, you should view interim-period statements with caution. Statements for internal purposes may not be prepared with the same rigour as those that accompany tax returns.

Is the business making or losing money?

At this stage, the purpose of reviewing the income statement is to find out whether the business is making money. To put it in the most basic terms, if sales or revenues are greater than expenses and costs, the net income is positive and the business is profitable.

If the owner works in the business, you will want to know whether or not he or she is paying him or herself a reasonable salary. When a business is not doing well, owners may forego paying themselves. If the profit disappears when a reasonable salary for the owner is deducted, the business is not profitable. It may accomplish the goal of giving the owner a satisfying job, but that doesn't make it a good investment. Potential buyers may want to "buy themselves a job," but they should be aware of what they are letting themselves in for. After all, someone with the skills to run a business can usually find a job without paying for one.

In *Chapter 2*, a seller was asking $500,000 for a business that the valuator considered to be worth no more than $250,000. Before the valuator talked his client out of it, the client seriously considered buying the business, even though it was over-priced. His rationale was that the business would pay him a salary of $100,000 a year, and he'd have his money back in five years. He was earning the same salary in his current position and was confident that he could continue to do so for the foreseeable future. What could be wrong with his analysis? Well, if the client stayed at his current job for the next five years he would earn a total of $500,000 in salary anyway. On top of that, he would still have the $500,000 that he hadn't shelled out for the business, and any investment income it may have generated. By not buying the business he would be better off financially — and, quite possibly, would sleep better at night too.

Business owners need to consider the value of their time and effort separate from their financial investment in the business, otherwise they may be short-changing themselves. Of course, one of the main reasons for buying a business is "to be my own boss," and that is as good a reason as any. Just don't let that cloud your judgment on how much to pay for a business.

Another complication is that while a business may appear profitable, those profits may not materialize if it is unable to collect on the sales it has made. In most cases, financial statements must be prepared under the accrual method of accounting, which means, among other things, that sales or revenue are recorded in the financial statements when customers are billed, rather than when they pay. Amounts that customers owe but have not yet been collected are recorded as accounts receivable. Be sure to review the accounts receivable for any significant overdue amounts. If any are ultimately uncollectible, they will increase bad debt expense, reducing net income.

Small business owners sometimes run personal expenses through the business. These may include vehicle costs, travel, meals and entertainment that are personal rather than business-related, and sometimes salaries to family members who are not active in the business. Although the CRA frowns on personal expenses being deducted from business income, it does happen. An owner may try to make the case to a prospective buyer that the business is profitable before the non-business expenses. That may be the case, but it could be difficult to prove. In any case, would you take the word of someone who has just admitted to breaking the CRA's rules?

Review the business's cash situation by examining its current balance sheet, if available, or its bank statements. If the business is low on cash and there is no reasonable explanation, such as the low point of a seasonal cycle, this could also be a sign of trouble. We'll come back to the business's financial information in more detail in coming chapters.

The economy

Economic conditions have an impact on a business's current operations and future outlook. When the economy is buoyant, consumers are more likely to buy and lenders are more likely to lend. During economic downturns, small businesses may face challenges on a number of fronts. Economic factors to consider include:

1. ***Interest rates.*** Businesses with significant debt are more sensitive to interest-rate changes, both up and down.

2. ***Availability of financing.*** Businesses that require new or additional financing during times of credit tightening may struggle to find it at a reasonable cost.

3. ***Fuel and energy prices.*** Changes in fuel and energy prices can have a big impact on businesses like food trucks, moving companies, transport and delivery services, greenhouses, and many manufacturers.

4. ***Exchange rates.*** Businesses that source from or sell to other countries may be affected by swings in currency exchange rates.

5. ***Minimum wage rates.*** Businesses that rely on low-wage employees may incur higher costs if legislated minimum wage rates rise.

6. ***Unemployment rate.*** Businesses are likely to find it difficult and more costly to hire staff as the unemployment rate falls. Conversely, rising unemployment typically makes recruiting easier, with less upward pressure on wages.

7. ***Commercial vacancy rates.*** Businesses facing lease renewals or requiring new premises may face higher or lower rental rates and property prices, depending on overall economic conditions.

Which valuation method will it be?

Once you have a good understanding of the industry, the business itself and the economy, you will have a much better sense of the outlook for the business, and whether it has the resources needed to continue operating for the foreseeable future. Everything you've learned about the business so far factors into your conclusion. Is it in an industry with a future? Does the business make money? Necessary resources include cash to operate, access to financing if needed, ability to attract employees, and an assured supply of raw materials and other inputs. We call a business that meets these criteria — that will continue to operate and has the resources to do so — a "going concern."

A business that has the resources to continue operating is a "going concern."

If a business is a going concern, the expectation is that it will keep generating cash — by selling its products or services — and/or that the value of the business will appreciate. All else being equal, a business that is a going concern is usually worth more than one that isn't.

If a business is not a going concern, the only way to get money out of it may be to cease operations and sell everything that it owns, in other words to liquidate it. The owner may not be planning to wind up the business — perhaps he or she is hoping for a turnaround — but it's not worth more, at that point in time, than they could get by liquidating it. An owner who chooses to continue operating an unprofitable business may end up no further ahead than if he or she ceased operations and sold everything that the business owns. If the business incurs debt to continue operating, its financial condition may deteriorate even further.

The determination whether a business is a going concern should drive the choice of a valuation method. When a business is not a going concern, its value is tied to how much its assets — the things that it owns — can be sold for. In this case, an asset-based valuation method would be appropriate. For businesses that are going concerns, you need to look beyond the value of the assets to the cash that the business is likely to generate in the future either from operations and/or when it is sold. In that case, a cash flow valuation method would be more appropriate.

Choosing a Valuation Method

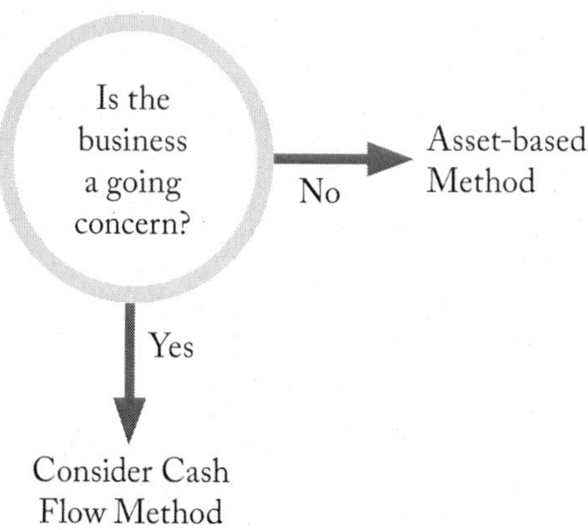

There may be times when you want to buy a business that is not a going concern. Perhaps the current owners have not been able to turn it around and it is on the verge of bankruptcy, but you have ideas, resources, contacts or other means to revive it. However, what you plan to bring to the business should not factor into what it is worth before you buy it. If the previous owners were not able to sustain a profitable business, then it shouldn't be valued as if it were one.

Let's look at how Joe, Mike and Elle might settle on a suitable valuation method. Joe's company, Niche Power, which manufacturers and distributes power conversion equipment, had $1.5 million of sales and net income of $120,000 in its most recent year. Joe pays himself a market-rate salary, the accounts receivable are current, and the company has a solid cash position. The outlook for the industry is positive; there is nothing to suggest that the business will not continue to operate, and it has the resources to do so. Niche Power is clearly a going concern, suggesting that a cash flow valuation method would be appropriate.

Blind Ninja, the blind-installation business, had revenues of $170,000 for its recently completed year, and net income before taxes of $96,000. Bill, the owner, considers $70,000 a reasonable salary for the work he does in the business. Therefore, the business generates $26,000 after deducting a reasonable salary. Bill does not charge personal expenses to the business. Construction in British Columbia is booming, and Blind Ninja has $100,000 of contracts lined up for the next six months. Blind Ninja also has all the hallmarks of a going concern, again lending itself to a cash flow valuation method.

Elle is in a less comfortable position. She has spent $25,000 and invested a considerable amount of time on developing the Poker Head game. With no sales and insufficient resources to continue, Poker Head is not yet a going concern, suggesting that an asset-based valuation method would be appropriate.

The choice of valuation method is never set in stone. As you learn more about a business, you may decide that another method is more appropriate. Upon closer examination, a business that may have initially appeared to be a going concern may turn out not to be, and vice versa. As we shall see later, even when a cash flow valuation method is more appropriate, calculating the value using the asset-based method provides very useful information. Let's look at each of these more closely, starting with the asset-based method.

6

The Asset-based Method: A Good Place to Start

As its name suggests, the asset-based valuation method centres on how much the assets of the business are worth. The starting point is to look at the assets on the financial statements. If the business is incorporated, those statements must include a balance sheet, which lists the business's assets and its liabilities. If a business is a sole proprietorship the assets used in the business are owned directly by the proprietor, and may be inseparable from his or her own personal assets. Although a balance sheet will likely not be prepared, the proprietor should be able to provide a list of assets used in the business.

The value of a business using the asset-based method is simply the business's total assets at their current value, less both asset selling costs and total liabilities.

With the asset-based method, we assume that if the business's assets are sold and its liabilities paid, the amount of money remaining is what the business is worth. This remaining amount represents the owner's equity in the business. It is the same concept as a homeowner's equity: how much a homeowner would end up with after selling his or her home (the asset), paying the real estate commission and any other costs associated with the sale (selling costs), and paying off the mortgage (the liability). Another term for owner's equity is "net assets," the assets net of liabilities.

When a business is a proprietorship, typically only the assets, and not the liabilities, are transferred to a new owner. As a result, the calculation is simpler: assets at current value less the selling costs equals net asset value.

Asset values

The dollar amount of assets as recorded on the balance sheet does not necessarily reflect their current value. Initially, assets are recorded at cost. Some assets, including buildings, equipment and vehicles, are subsequently "written down" over a period of time to recognize their diminishing value as they are used. The accounting term for this systematic writedown is "depreciation" or "amortization."

Let's use Niche Power, Joe's manufacturing and distribution business, as an example. The building that Niche Power owns cost $100,000 to build 10 years ago, has an estimated life of 20 years, and has been depreciated at a rate of $5,000 a year. The land that the building is located on was bought for $50,000 but, because land does not wear out with use, is not depreciated.

The remaining dollar amount of an asset on the balance sheet, after depreciation or amortization, is known as "book value." An informal term for a business's financial records is "the books." Book value, therefore, is the amount recorded in the books.

Niche Power's building has a book value of $50,000 (the $100,000 cost less depreciation of $5,000 for 10 years). The book value of the land and building combined is $100,000 ($50,000 building plus $50,000 for the land). Real estate values in the Toronto area have skyrocketed over the past

10 years, to the point where the market value of the land and the building is now $200,000. We use this current value, rather than the book value of $100,000, to value the business.

When an asset's current value is less than its book value, we say that the asset is impaired (no, not drunk). A basic principle of accounting is conservatism, so when there is a choice of values — book value or current value — choosing the one that results in the lower asset amount is required. Thus, in the case of an impaired asset, Generally Accepted Accounting Principles (GAAP) require us to write down the asset to the current value. Bear in mind, though, that not all small businesses prepare financial statements according to GAAP, and thus such write-downs may not have been done.

In addition, while GAAP allows for assets to be written up to their current value in certain circumstances, the conditions for doing so can be onerous — namely, that the current value can be reliably measured and must be reviewed annually. As a result, most small businesses will not go through the exercise required to write assets up. Typically, the amount recorded on the balance sheet is the asset's book value, unless the current value is less than book value, in which case it may be written down to the lower amount.

With the asset-based valuation method, assets are adjusted to their current value. Here are some considerations in determining the current value of typical assets in a small business:

1. ***Cash.*** The easiest asset to value! It's worth its stated amount.

2. ***Accounts receivable.*** Review the list of accounts receivable for any amounts not paid by their due date. In some cases, there may be a reasonable explanation — for example, a good customer who is consistently

late but ultimately pays. If not, consider a reduction for amounts that may not be collected. As well, a receivable that is due sometime in the future is worth less than one due immediately. For example, a receivable collected today could be deposited in an interest-earning account. The value of a long-term receivable should be discounted to reflect the interest that could have been earned.

3. ***Prepaid expenses.*** These may include security deposits or advances paid for services not yet delivered. Their current value is often the recorded amount. If prepaid expenses include unused supplies, consider whether those items have value to a new owner. For example, if a new owner plans to change the price of the business's products or services, old brochures probably no longer have any value.

4. ***Inventory.*** Obsolete or slow-moving inventory may need to be written down to reflect how much it can realistically be sold for.

5. ***Work-in-progress.*** Ensure any profit that has been included for works in progress is only for the percentage of the project completed at that point. The total profit for a project should be included only if all its costs have also been accounted for.

6. ***Furniture and office equipment.*** The current value of used furniture, even if relatively new, may be significantly less than its purchase price.

7. ***Machinery and equipment.*** The value of equipment can also fall rapidly after purchase. Appraisals may be needed to determine current value.

8. ***Real estate.*** There can be a significant difference between a property's current value and book value. An appraisal of the property's current value should be obtained from a real estate agent or appraiser. A real

estate appraiser, as an unbiased third party, may be more objective, but will charge a fee.

9. ***Leasehold improvements.*** Any leasehold improvements on the balance sheet are enhancements that the business has paid for as the tenant of the leased space. These can include painting, flooring, cabinetry, shelving, lighting and partitions. Leasehold improvements are initially recorded at cost and then amortized over the term of the lease and possibly renewal periods. Leasehold improvements by their nature cannot be easily extracted from the leased premises. If the buyer of a business intends to remain in the leased premises, the improvements may have value. On the other hand, if the purchaser plans to renovate the leased premises, the existing fixtures and other items may have little or no value. As well, costs may be incurred to remove these items.

10. ***Investments.*** A small business may invest surplus cash in stocks, bonds and other marketable securities. The current value of such investments can usually be easily determined by obtaining statements from the financial institutions where they are held.

11. ***Intangible assets.*** These are assets that are not physical in nature, and include patents, royalties, licences, copyrights, software, and intellectual property. If they can be sold separately from the business, they may have value in their own right. If a business is not a going concern, they typically have minimal value. Intangible assets are notoriously difficult to value. *Chapter 12 — Early-stage Intangible Assets* offers further guidance.

12. ***Shareholder loans and advances receivable.*** These are amounts borrowed by the owner from the business and not yet repaid. Typically, they are deducted from the selling price of the business.

13. ***Tax losses.*** A company that has incurred losses may have an asset on its balance sheet described as tax losses. If the company becomes profitable in the future, these tax losses could be set off against future income taxes. If you are buying a business with a view to using its tax losses, you should consult a tax adviser.

An asset's current value will typically fall within a range. Choosing the appropriate value in the range depends on the circumstances of the business being valued. If the business is in trouble or on the verge of bankruptcy, its owners may be forced to act quickly or accept a lower price than would otherwise be the case. We call this scenario a "forced liquidation" and we would use "liquidation values" at the lower end of the range. If the business is not facing imminent doom, current values on the higher end of the range would likely be more appropriate.

Asset selling costs

If a business sells its assets bit by bit, it is likely to incur various costs such as sales commissions, broker and legal fees, and sales taxes. If, instead, the owner sells the entire business as a single package, including all the assets, these selling costs might be avoided. When valuing a business under a forced-liquidation scenario, it may be reasonable to deduct selling costs, given the very real prospect that the assets will have to be sold piecemeal if a buyer for the business as a whole is not found. As a buyer, you can use this knowledge to your advantage and offer no more for the business than the seller might get by selling the assets individually. If there is no immediate plan or pressure to wind up the business, deducting asset selling costs may not be a reasonable assumption.

Liabilities

In most cases, the current value of a liability is the amount recorded on the balance sheet. Exceptions include loans or long-term debt. If the long-term debt carries a higher rate of interest than could be currently negotiated — i.e. not at "market rate" — it is reasonable to assume that the debt will be paid off and replaced with debt at market rates. But doing so may result in prepayment penalties, which should be added to the liabilities.

Remember to take into account liabilities incurred since the last financial statements were prepared. Assets are less of a concern, as sellers are likely to include all of them. Liabilities are more prone to be overlooked. As well, fees may have been incurred, but not yet billed, for lawyers, accountants and other professionals who have helped prepare the business for sale. These fees should be included with liabilities if they are to be paid through the business.

A business may have potential liabilities that are not recorded in the financial statements because they are contingent on the outcome of a future event. For example, if a former employee sues a company for wrongful dismissal, the company has a contingent liability. However, only if the company is found guilty will it have an actual liability. The very nature of contingent liabilities sometimes makes it difficult to know whether they will become liabilities — and if so, at what amount. For this reason, contingent liabilities are often not included in liabilities when determining the value of a business. Instead, the buyer may insist on holding back a portion of the purchase price until the issue is resolved.

Going concerns

We mentioned earlier that the asset-based valuation method is most appropriate for businesses that are not going concerns. An exception is those businesses whose value is inextricably tied to their assets, even though they are going concerns. Holding companies, for example, are often set up to hold a basket of investments, such as stocks, bonds, mutual funds, real estate or even investments in other companies. Holding companies may earn income from their investments but not have operations of their own.

An acquaintance has a company that owns three small apartment buildings. Other than a modest profit that it earns from rents, the company has no other income, nor any operations or employees. It has the resources and intent to continue operating, so it is a going concern. The value of the company, however, depends entirely on the value of the three apartment buildings. As a result, if the owner were thinking of selling the company, an asset-based valuation method would be appropriate using the buildings' current market value.

The first step in any business valuation should be to calculate the net asset value. However, for most going concerns that's only the beginning of the process.

Even when a business is a going concern best suited to a cash flow valuation method, the net asset value should still be calculated. A going concern can be worth significantly more than its net asset value, but it is unlikely to be worth less. The net asset value thus serves a useful purpose. It provides a minimum floor for the value for the business, as well as information to assess risk, which, as we will see later, is a component of cash flow valuation methods.

With that in mind, let's add a few steps to our valuation process on the next page:

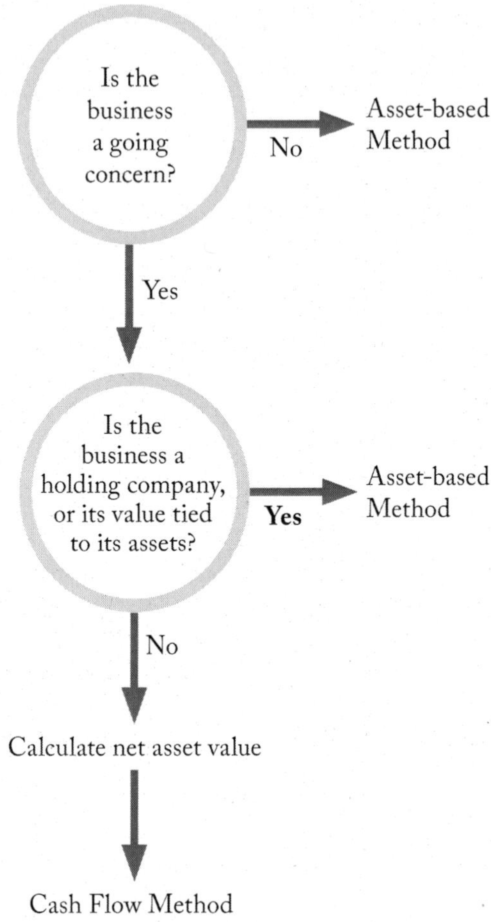

Calculating net asset value

Niche Power

Let's use Joe's company, Niche Power, the manufacturer and distributor of power conversion equipment, to explain the asset-based valuation method. Here is the company's latest balance sheet, prepared by Joe's CPA one month ago:

Niche Power – Balance Sheet

Assets		
Cash		$ 40,000
Accounts receivable		$ 50,000
Inventory		$ 60,000
Land & building – at cost	$ 150,000	
Accumulated depreciation	$ (50,000)	
Land & building – book value		$ 100,000
Total Assets		**$ 250,000**
Liabilities		
Accounts payable		$ 30,000
Bank loan		$ 20,000
Total Liabilities		**$ 50,000**
Shareholders' Equity		
Share capital		$ 1,000
Retained earnings		$ 199,000
Shareholders' Equity		**$ 200,000**
Total Liabilities and Shareholders' Equity		**$ 250,000**

We start with Niche Power's total assets of $250,000 as recorded on the balance sheet, and then adjust them to their current values as follows:

- Accounts receivable had been reduced by a $2,000 bad-debt provision. As these accounts were collected after the financial statements were prepared, the provision is not needed and has been added back. There are no other overdue accounts.
- An inventory review revealed $2,000 of product that is obsolete and no longer sellable. The inventory has been reduced by this amount.
- As noted earlier, the current market value of the land and building

is $200,000. We replace the book value of $100,000 with the current value.

- Because Niche Power is a going concern, selling costs on the assets have not been deducted.

Then, from the total assets restated to their current value, we deduct the liabilities. As we noted earlier, typically the liabilities on the balance sheet are already at their current value. Let's assume this is the case for Niche Power and the current value of the liabilities is $50,000.

The net asset value of Niche Power, after the above adjustments, is $300,000.

Total assets per the balance sheet	$ 250,000
Adjustments:	
Bad debt provision not needed	$ 2,000
Inventory writedown	$ (2,000)
Land and building	
Current value $200,000	
Book value ($100,000)	$ 100,000
Total current value of assets	$ 350,000
Deduct the liabilities	$ (50,000)
Net asset value	**$ 300,000**

How does the net asset value of $300,000 compare to the shareholders' equity on the balance sheet before the adjustments? The shareholders' equity on Niche Power's balance sheet is $200,000, representing the assets at book value less the liabilities. When assets are adjusted to their current value, we have an increase of $100,000. This increase highlights why it is important to consider the current values of assets and not simply their book value as recorded on the balance sheet.

Blind Ninja

Blind Ninja is a proprietorship. The business assets — a van and tools used to install blinds — are therefore included with the owner Bill's personal assets. Bill has offered to sell Mike 50 percent of the business for $30,000. Bill has suggested that he incorporate a company and transfer the van and tools to it. The van has a current value of $19,000 and the tools are worth $1,000. Let's keep it simple and assume that any accounts payable, bank loans or other liabilities in respect of Blind Ninja will be taken care of by Bill before the new company is formed. Blind Ninja has installation projects of $100,000 lined up. The net asset value of the new company, after Mike's contribution of $30,000, is shown below.

Van current value	$	19,000
Tools	$	1,000
Cash from Mike	$	30,000
Total net assets	**$**	**50,000**

I have not included the $100,000 in upcoming projects. Until the work is done, this cannot be classified as an asset. As well, Blind Ninja will need to incur labour costs to earn revenue from these projects. Since Blind Ninja is a going concern, selling costs on the assets have not been deducted.

Since Bill is offering to sell a 50 percent interest in his business, Mike's share of the net assets of $50,000 would be $25,000. Bill is asking $30,000 for an interest that would be backed by $25,000 of assets. Is this reasonable? Because we know that Blind Ninja is a going concern, Mike has every reason to expect a return on his investment in the business from future cash flow, and not just from what could be realized by selling the assets. Therefore, it seems reasonable to ask Mike to pay more than the net asset value. We will discuss how much more when we look at the cash flow method of valuation.

Poker Head

The only tangible asset that Elle uses in her business is a computer, which is of minimal value. But there is an intangible asset — the brand name, the art and the code, collectively known as the "intellectual property" — that is Poker Head. Elle has spent $25,000, the amount she paid Cole to develop the game demo, and has invested a considerable amount of her time. Still, that does not mean that Poker Head is worth at least $25,000. It could be worth considerably more if the game has potential. Conversely, it could have little value if there is no demand for the game. Poker Head's net asset value hinges on the value of the intellectual property comprising the game. We'll take a closer look at how to value early-stage intangible assets in *Chapter 12.*

The asset-based valuation method is relatively easy to apply, when the assets are tangible, and, as mentioned earlier, the net asset value should be determined for any business being valued. Doing so gives us an amount that the business is worth at its very least. However, for most businesses that are going concerns we can't stop there. Going concerns, by their nature, have the potential to produce cash flow above and beyond what one could realize by selling their assets. The next few chapters on cash flow methods are more complicated, but also the most important.

7

Cash Flow Method: Often the Way to Go

For businesses that are going concerns — those that will continue to operate and have the resources to do so — the expectation is that cash will be generated on a regular basis from selling products or services. The total future cash flow could be significantly more than the business would realize by selling its assets. For example, Blind Ninja had net assets of $20,000 (before Mike's investment) and $26,000 in net income in its latest financial year, after deducting a reasonable salary for the owner, Bill. If it keeps going at the same rate, Blind Ninja will generate more cash in less than a year than it could bring in by selling the assets.

The first step in determining the value of a business using a cash flow method is to estimate the cash that will come from the business.

Expected cash flow

Cash flow is the change in cash from one period, often a year, to another. While past performance is not a guarantee of future results, it is a useful starting point. Historical cash flows can help predict the pattern and amount of future ones. The cash flow for prior periods can usually be calculated by analyzing the business's financial statements.

Financial statements prepared according to Generally Accepted Accounting Principles (GAAP) include a "cash flow statement." But this statement is not in a format that readily lends itself to the information we need. The purpose of this GAAP cash flow statement is to show the change in a company's cash position over a period of time, typically from one year-end to the next. It is divided into three parts — cash flow from operations, investing, and financing activities — and is compiled from information in the balance sheet and income statements. For our purposes, using the actual balance sheet and income statement, rather than a statement derived from them, will give us more detailed information in the format that we need. Due to cost, many small businesses opt to prepare financial statements to a lesser standard than GAAP and, therefore, will not prepare this type of cash flow statement anyway.

Let's start with the income statement. Net income or net earnings — often simply called profit — is not the same as cash flow. Even when financial statements are prepared to a lesser standard than GAAP, the Canada Revenue Agency requires businesses (other than farming, fishing, or self-employed commissioned sales agents) to use the "accrual" basis of accounting. The main difference between accrual and cash basis accounting is in the timing of when revenue and expenses are recognized. With cash basis accounting, revenue is recorded when cash is received, and expenses when they are paid. Accrual accounting records revenue when it is earned, even if no cash has been received. Likewise, it records expenses when they are incurred, even if they have not been paid.

Using accrual accounting, if Blind Ninja lands a $10,000 blind-installation job, it will record the revenue on completion of the project. Using cash basis accounting, it will not account for the revenue until the customer pays. Expenses are treated the same way. In the case of accrual accounting, if Blind Ninja receives an invoice for $500 of supplies, it records the expense on receipt of the invoice. But cash basis accounting records the amount when the invoice is actually paid, even if that is months later.

The advantage of accrual accounting is that it better matches revenue and expenses to the periods in which they are incurred, allowing an owner to assess more accurately whether the business is profitable. Cash basis accounting can make a business appear profitable simply by delaying payment of expenses. Accrual accounting solves this timing problem. When valuing a business using a cash flow method, we want the benefit of accrual accounting, i.e. matching revenues with expenses. We therefore start with the income statement, and then make adjustments for what we call "non-cash" items (described later).

Only cash, and not accounting net income, can ultimately be distributed to business owners.

A good starting point is to analyze income statements for the past two to four years. A review of these statements and discussions with management will help determine which year, or combination of years, are most relevant for estimating future cash flow. If the business has recently undergone big changes — for example, a plant closure or a successful new product line — only the most recent year's income statement may present an accurate picture of its financial outlook. An average of several prior years may be more appropriate if the business is cyclical from one year to the next — for example, a ski rental business that has to contend with winters with little snow. As we mentioned earlier, business valuation is as much an art as a science. So use the historical period that, in your judgment, is the best indicator of future results.

Forecasts or budgets, if the business has prepared them, may also provide useful information. It is important to keep in mind that you are valuing the business at the present time, not at some date in the future. If future results depend on resources that are not yet in place, the cash flow calculation should not include those results. For example, Mike's contacts in China make it possible that Blind Ninja will some day supply the blinds that it installs. But the firm is not currently a supplier of blinds, and it is not reasonable to value the business as if it were. As well, Blind Ninja will need additional financing for the initial order of blinds and to meet other costs involved in this new line of business.

Our goal is to determine the annual expected — or "sustainable" — cash flow of the business as it is. We want to make a reasonable assumption of how much cash the business can generate in a typical year, based on the resources it has right now. We assume that the expected cash flow will continue for some years, and discuss that later. For now, focusing on a single year's cash flow allows us to more readily compare the business to the expected return from other types of investments.

After picking the income statement for the periods that appear to be the best indicator of future results, the next step is to adjust for various items.

1. Non-cash items

The accounting principles used to determine net income are not always cash based. In order to focus on cash flow, we need to adjust net income for typical accounting entries that do not reflect actual cash transactions. These include:

- Depreciation and amortization expense, which is the systematic write-down of assets to reflect their diminishing value, is an accounting entry, not a cash transaction. For example, let's assume that Niche Power bought a $100 office chair. Each year it records $10 of depreciation expense. Adding this expense back to net income allows us to focus on cash flow. Assets such as equipment and machinery used in operations wear out and may need to be replaced periodically. We will return later to dealing with the cost of replacing assets.

- The income statement may include gains or losses on the sale or disposal of assets. These are typically assets that the business uses in its operations, but does not sell to customers in the normal course of business. Because gains and losses are based on the book value of the asset — the original cost less any depreciation or amortization — they do not reflect the actual cash impact of the transaction. Let's assume that Niche Power bought that $100 chair five years ago, and it has been depreciated to a book value of $50. If Niche Power sells the chair this year for $60, the gain for accounting purposes would be $10 (selling price of $60 less the book value of $50). But the cash that came in during the year for the transaction is $60, not $10. Removing gains or losses from the income statement allows us to focus on the cash flow from normal operations. Because gains increase net income, they are deducted; conversely, losses, which lower net income, are added back.

2. Income taxes

Because we are looking at the business as an investment, net income before tax makes it easier to compare it to other investments that are typically evaluated on a pre-tax basis. So even though income taxes are inescapable and inevitable, we add them back to net income in order to focus on pre-tax cash flow.

3. Financing

A business can be financed in many ways: bank loans, lines of credit, long-term debt or additional capital from owners. A new owner may choose to finance the business in a different way from previous practice. He or she may opt to repay existing debt with additional capital, or replace existing financing with a lower cost alternative. Therefore, we do not include financing considerations as part of regular business operations. Excluding interest expense also makes it easier to compare one business to another, and to other investments.

4. EBITDA

You will recall the rule-of-thumb method that multiplied EBITDA (earnings before interest, income taxes, depreciation and amortization) by some number. The rationale for using EBITDA instead of net income is that, with the exception of gains and losses, the adjustments we mentioned above are already taken into account. However, using EBITDA does not take into account other important considerations. Let's press ahead and see what other adjustments should be considered.

5. Reflect the future

We started with historical net income, but because our focus is on the future, our next step is to adjust for revenues and expenses that will be different in the future. Items to consider include:

- Revenues and expenses for discontinued products or services should be removed.
- If products or services were added or removed partway through a year, adjust revenues and expenses to reflect what they would be for a full year going forward.
- Expenses for unusual events or those not expected to recur — such as fire or flood damage, lawsuits, severance pay, and relocation costs — should be added back.
- If prices or rates have changed, adjust revenues and expenses to the rates that will prevail in the future — for example, salary increases, lower fuel prices or higher material costs.
- If a business sells to or buys from related entities, consider whether these

transactions are at market rates. A great discount on items supplied by the current owner's brother may not be available to a new owner.

- We assume that the expected cash flow continues each year for an indefinite period. In order to sustain that cash flow, however, operating assets such as vehicles, machinery and equipment may need to be replaced. The average annual cost of replacing these assets in the future should be deducted.

By focusing on expected annual cash flow, we have factored in growth only for the coming year. We will address growth for future years at a later step in the valuation process.

6. Non-business items

The distinction between a small business owner and the business itself can be a bit blurry. Owners may make decisions about the business for non-business reasons. The following should be reviewed:

- The salary an owner pays herself or himself, and possibly other family members, may not reflect either the time spent, or be at market rates — in other words, what it would cost to hire someone else to do the same job. Some owners may pay themselves more than market rates, but others may pay less, especially if the business cannot afford to match them. When valuing a business, we look at it as an entity separate from its owner and, therefore, we need to adjust the owner's salary to market rates.
- As we noted earlier, a prospective buyer may be interested in a business in order to buy himself a job. Even then, a market-rate salary should be used in the valuation, not the prospective owner's planned salary. Keep in mind that a business that makes money only if the owner doesn't pay himself or herself a market-rate salary, is not a profitable business.

- Examine the income statement for expenses not related to the business. Although the Canada Revenue Agency does not allow businesses to deduct personal expenses for tax purposes, some do. Owners sometimes have their businesses pay for personal trips, meals, entertainment, and vehicle costs. If it is possible to identify which expenses are personal — and that may be difficult — add them back.

7. Redundant assets

Assets that are not essential to a business's operations are considered "redundant." For example, a business may own equipment or real estate that it no longer uses. These assets may earn income if they are rented out, but that income should not be considered part of the business's regular operations. Prospective buyers will not likely pay top dollar for such assets. Redundant assets can usually be sold separately from the business, with the seller realizing more money in total by doing so. *Chapter 10 — Redundant Assets* provides an example.

Assets used in operations can also be redundant if the business has other options. For example, Niche Power owns the land and building that it uses in its manufacturing operations. However, the facilities are not highly specialized and Niche Power could easily move to another location. Joe is considering keeping the property when he sells his business, and leasing it either to the new owner or to someone else.

Ideally, a business owner removes redundant assets before talks with potential buyers. If that has not been done, the valuation should take this into account. Because redundant assets are not part of regular business operations, any revenues and expenses attributable to them should be removed from net income when calculating expected cash flow. Review the balance sheet to identify assets that may be redundant, paying special attention to the following:

- Equipment no longer used in operations. Add back any related expenses such as insurance, maintenance and storage.
- Real estate not used in operations. Deduct any rental revenue and add back expenses such as property taxes, insurance, repairs, and maintenance.
- Equipment or real estate used in operations that can be rented or leased instead. Add back expenses as noted above, and deduct the cost of renting or leasing.
- Obsolete inventory. Add back expenses on inventory that cannot be sold, such as storage costs.
- Surplus vehicles. Add back insurance, fuel, maintenance and leasing costs for vehicles that are not needed or are used for personal rather than business purposes.
- Cash or securities not needed for the business. A business may have invested surplus cash, rather than distributed it to owners. Deduct income from these investments.
- Loans or advances to owners. Deduct interest income from these loans, as we would for other debt.

In summary: To determine expected cash flow, we start with net income and then adjust for non-cash items including depreciation, amortization and gains or losses; income taxes, financing costs, and non-business expenses; changes to revenue or expenses that will be different in the future; and the effect of redundant assets.

Bearing all this in mind, let's calculate the expected cash flow for Niche Power and Blind Ninja.

Niche Power

After reviewing income statements for the past four years and after discussions with Joe, the latest year's income statement, below, was considered the best indicator of future results.

Niche Power – Income Statement

Sales	**$**	**1,500,000**
Cost of goods sold	$	(900,000)
Gross profit	$	600,000
Expenses		
Salaries and office costs	$	(417,000)
Depreciation	$	(5,000)
Interest	$	(1,000)
Bad debts	$	(2,000)
Property tax	$	(3,000)
	$	(428,000)
Net income before taxes	$	172,000
Income taxes	$	(52,000)
Net Income	**$**	**120,000**

To convert net income to expected cash flow, the following adjustments were made.

- Depreciation, a non-cash item, was added back.
- Income taxes were added back to evaluate the cash flow on a pre-tax basis.
- Interest expense was added back to focus on business operations, irrespective of financing.
- Salary and office costs included $1,000 for a celebration to honour a long-time employee's retirement. Since this is not expected to recur, it was added back.
- Bad-debt expense of $2,000 was added back because the account for which it had been provided for was subsequently collected.

- The land and building is considered a redundant asset because the business could easily move to other rented premises. If the property were removed from Niche Power, the property tax of $3,000 would not be incurred, and is thus added back. The estimated $14,000 cost of renting other premises was deducted.

Niche Power – Cash Flow Calculation

Net Income	**$**	**120,000**
Adjustments:		
Depreciation	$	5,000
Income taxes	$	52,000
Interest	$	1,000
Celebration	$	1,000
Bad debt	$	2,000
Property tax	$	3,000
Building rental	$	(14,000)
	$	50,000
Expected Cash Flow	**$**	**170,000**

No other adjustments were needed. A review of the balance sheet did not reveal any other redundant assets, Joe pays himself a market-rate salary, and no personal expenses were charged to the business. No equipment or machinery is used in the business other than small tools, and their annual replacement cost is included in cost of goods sold. Niche Power's expected annual cash flow, after adjustments, is thus $170,000, as shown.

Blind Ninja

Blind Ninja is a less complicated example. The blind-installation services are performed at customers' sites and the rest of the operations — sales and accounting — are done from Bill's home. Again, the latest year's net income below, was considered the best indicator of future results. Because

Blind Ninja is a sole proprietorship, the total net income of $96,000 would be included on Bill's personal tax return.

Blind Ninja – Income Statement

Revenue	$	170,000
Expenses:		
Employee wages	$	(60,000)
Office & vehicle	$	(10,000)
Depreciation	$	(4,000)
Total expenses	$	(74,000)
Net income before taxes	**$**	**96,000**

To convert net income to cash flow the following adjustments are required:

- Depreciation of $4,000 is added back, as this is a non-cash item.
- The salary expense includes the salary paid to the sole employee, Mike, but not a salary for the owner, Bill. A reasonable salary of $70,000 for Bill, who works full time in the business, is deducted.

No other adjustments need to be made. Because we are starting with net income before taxes, there are no taxes to add back. There are no redundant assets, and no personal expenses were charged to the business. The vehicle used in the business will eventually need to be replaced, but Bill and Mike have agreed that they will buy any new vehicles personally. Therefore, equipment replacement costs have not been deducted. As shown, Blind Ninja's expected annual cash flow, after adjustments, is $30,000.

Blind Ninja – Expected Cash Flow

Net income before taxes	**$**	**96,000**
Adjustments:		
Depreciation	$	4,000
Reasonable owner salary	$	(70,000)
Expected Cash Flow	**$**	**30,000**

Now that we have worked out the expected cash flows, the next step is to use these numbers to value the businesses.

8

The Multiple: A Critical Number

How do we use expected cash flow to come up with the total value of a business? The process is similar to the rule-of-thumb method, where we multiplied EBITDA by some number, except that instead of EBITDA we use expected cash flow. We call the number that we multiply cash flow by "the multiple." The result of this calculation — cash flow times the multiple — we refer to as "capitalized" cash flow. While there are many definitions of "capitalize" (including to print in capital letters), for our purposes, we will go with the Collins English dictionary: "To compute the present value of a business from actual or potential earnings." In this case, we substitute "potential earnings" with expected cash flow, and to "compute" the value of the business we apply the multiple.

The big question is: What multiple should we pick? Why a multiple of five and not four? Since the higher the multiple, the higher the perceived value of the business, this is like asking why one buyer would pay more for a business than another. Let's assume that both Buyer A and Buyer B have calculated a business's expected cash flow at $20,000. Buyer A is willing to pay a multiple of five times cash flow, resulting in a total value of $100,000. Buyer B is willing to pay only four times cash flow, for a value of $80,000.

	Buyer A	Buyer B
Expected cash flow	$ 20,000	$ 20,000
Multiple	x 5	x 4
Willing to pay	$ 100,000	$ 80,000

Why the difference? There could be any number of explanations. Perhaps Buyer A sees more potential in the business, and is confident that the cash flow will be higher than expected. As a result, he is willing to pay more. On the other hand, Buyer B may see the business as a riskier proposition, and is worried that the cash flow will fall short of $20,000. To mitigate that risk, Buyer B is inclined to pay less. We'll discuss the factors that go into choosing a multiple in more detail later in this chapter.

The relationship between the multiple and a rate of return

Readers may be more familiar with the concept of a "rate of return" than with a multiple. If you earn interest on a savings account or a similar investment, that interest rate is the rate of return. If the interest rate on a term deposit is two percent a year, then the rate of return is two percent. As succinctly put by the Oxford Dictionary, a rate of return is:

"The annual income from an investment expressed as a proportion (usually a percentage) of the original investment."

What is the relationship between the rate of return (ROR) and a multiple? Answer: The multiple is the inverse, or opposite, of the rate of return. In other words, one (1) divided by the rate of return gives you the multiple and, conversely, one (1) divided by the multiple gives you the rate of return. Here are some examples:

1 divided by the ROR = multiple	1 divided by the multiple = ROR
1 ÷ 20% = 5	1 ÷ 5 = 20%
1 ÷ 25% = 4	1 ÷ 4 = 25%
1 ÷ 10% = 10	1 ÷ 10 = 10%

The choice of what multiple to use boils down, therefore, to deciding on an appropriate rate of return. Saying to a seller "I'll give you five times cash flow," means the same as "I'm looking for a 20 percent rate of return."

If Buyer A pays $100,000 for a business with an expected annual cash flow of $20,000, he is paying five times cash flow and his target rate of return is 20 percent (see calculation below). If Buyer B is willing to pay only four times cash flow or $80,000 for the same business, his expected rate of return is 25 percent. However, if Buyer B was right to be more skeptical and the cash flow ends up being only $16,000, his rate of return would also be 20 percent.

	Buyer A		Buyer B		Buyer B	
Amount paid	$	100,000	$	80,000	$	80,000
Cash flow	$	20,000	$	20,000	$	16,000
Cash flow/ Amount paid	$	20,000 ÷ 100,000	$	20,000 ÷ 80,000	$	16,000 ÷ 80,000
Rate of return		20%		25%		20%

Choosing a multiple, therefore, means the same as choosing a target rate of return. That begs the next question: What is an appropriate rate of return?

Risk-free rate

The rate of return is made up of two components: a risk-free rate and a risk premium. Let's start with the risk-free rate. Every investment carries a risk that you won't get all or some of your money back when expected. A risk-free investment is one where the risk of that happening is so low as to be negligible. Very few investments qualify for this status. Among those that do in Canada:

- Government of Canada bonds, which are guaranteed by the federal government. The risk of the government defaulting on these bonds is exceptionally low.
- Guaranteed income certificates (GICs), which are term deposits issued by banks and other financial institutions. These are protected by the Canada Deposit Insurance Corporation, a federal Crown corporation that guarantees eligible deposits to a maximum of $100,000. Deposits held at credit unions are protected by various provincial deposit insurance agencies to specified limits or, in some provinces, unlimited amounts. In the unlikely event that a financial institution or credit union defaults, investors would get their money back up to the maximum amount covered.
- High-yield savings accounts, subject to the same protection as GICs and term deposits, as above.

Based on the average interest rate on a five-year non-refundable GIC in 2017, let's assume a risk-free rate of two percent.

Risk premium

Although we may assume that the cash flow from a business that is a going concern will continue indefinitely, we can never take that for granted. Circumstances can, and often do, change. Consequently, the cash flow could be more than predicted, or it could be less, but rarely will it be exactly the same. If cash flows are more than expected, that's great; the concern, however, is that they will be less. For that reason alone, you should never invest in a business without expecting a return above and beyond what you could earn from putting your money into a risk-free investment. A business is not like a term deposit or GIC. Its value can evaporate quickly with little or no warning. What's more, you can't sell a business nearly as quickly as a GIC or a Government of Canada bond, which adds to the inherent risk.

When investors take on risk, they expect — quite naturally — to earn more than the risk-free rate. How much more depends on a how risky they perceive the investment to be, and on the level of risk they are willing to accept. The appetite for risk and the assessment of any particular risk often differs from one investor to the next. But all investors expect a higher rate of return for taking on greater risk. And small businesses are almost always considered riskier investments than large enterprises.

Small businesses are generally considered among the riskiest investments and thus buyers and investors typically expect high rates of return.

How do we decide what premium to add to the risk-free rate to take account of risk? Two businesses in the same sector may have identical cash flows, yet face different risks and prospects. An analysis of the sector, the businesses' individual strengths and weaknesses, and their exposure to broader economic trends offer some insight. These are the same three general areas that we looked at earlier in assessing whether the business was a going concern. Now we expand that analysis, with a few more considerations focused specifically on risk and growth potential.

Industry sector

We looked at growth prospects for the sector in our going concern analysis. Let's fine-tune that analysis and consider where on the growth spectrum — modest or high — the sector lies. Buyers of businesses in sectors with high growth potential may appear to be willing to accept a lower rate of return, putting a correspondingly higher value on the business. If the growth materializes and cash flow is more than expected, the buyer will end up with a higher rate of return.

Sectors with high barriers to entry — obstacles that make it difficult to enter the sector — tend to be less competitive. These obstacles can include significant startup costs, licensing requirements, tough government regulations, geographical constraints, and technology challenges. If a business faces little competition for the foreseeable future, there is less risk of cash flow falling short, and a lower rate of return may be acceptable.

Public companies are not directly comparable to small private businesses, as discussed in *Chapter 3 — Market Method*, but they can provide a window on a sector. A public company's price/earnings (P/E) ratio is the same concept as a multiple. The P/E ratio is the company's current share price divided by its annual earnings per share. Thus, a company trading at $10 per share with earnings per share of $1.25 would have a P/E ratio of 8 ($10 ÷ $1.25).

Some well-known business authors have expressed opinions on the relationship between a P/E ratio and a small business valuation. Andrew Heslop puts it this way in his book *How to Value and Sell Your Business*: "It has been suggested to me that the effective P/E ratio for a small private company could be 50 percent lower than that of a comparable publicly quoted company that operates in the same business sector, but of course this will not apply universally."

In *Valuing Your Business: Strategies to Maximize the Sale Price*, Frederick D. Lipman writes: "You cannot analogize a business worth less than $5 million with a business in the same industry worth over $50 million. The business over $50 million always sells for a higher multiplier..."

The business

Whatever you learn about the business in assessing whether it is a going concern is also useful in choosing an appropriate rate of return. Take into account the following factors:

1. ***Uniqueness.*** A business that is truly one of a kind may have a competitive advantage that justifies a lower rate of return. Attributes to look for are whether it offers a product or service that others do not; is difficult to imitate; has been "first out the gate" with a new product or service; or has a unique location.

2. ***Customers.*** A business with strong and broad customer relationships that is not dependent on a few customers — in other words, does not have all its eggs in one basket — has less risk.

3. ***Revenue contracts.*** A business that has guaranteed revenue through contracts for future sales has less risk.

4. ***Suppliers.*** A business that is not dependent on a single supplier has less risk.

5. ***Employees.*** A business that has a strong management team, a loyal pool of employees, and does not rely on one or two key individuals or skilled employees has less risk and more growth potential.

6. ***Assets.*** A business with substantial, saleable assets has less risk. In the

event the business goes under, the owners can recoup more of their investment if they can sell the machinery, office equipment or other assets.

7. ***Predictability.*** If revenues and net income have remained consistent over time, there may be less risk in predicted cash flows.

8. ***Growth Potential.*** Some buyers prefer to invest in a high-growth business and, as a result, they may be willing to accept a lower rate of return.

To the extent that the above factors are positive, reflecting lower business risk or higher growth potential, a lower rate of return may be acceptable. Conversely, investors are likely to demand a higher rate of return as the risk rises of not achieving expected cash flows.

By focusing on the immediate year's expected cash flow, we have not factored in the potential for future growth. If we include growth in the cash flows, the risk of not achieving projected cash flow is higher. Typically, it is easier to reflect growth potential in the rate of return: the more growth potential a business has, the lower the acceptable rate of return. In some cases, such as startup businesses, it may be preferable to include growth in cash flow and adjust the rate of return accordingly. We'll discuss that further in *Chapter 11 — Discounted Cash Flow.*

The economy

General economic conditions also play a role in determining an acceptable rate of return. Investors may have less appetite for risk if the economic outlook is uncertain or financial markets are in turmoil, as was the case in 2008. The opposite applies when the economy is booming. Financing may be more readily available during good times, making it easier to buy a business, attracting more buyers into the market, and perhaps lowering the targeted rate of return.

Financial markets also influence the risk-free rate. If the Bank of Canada raises or lowers its benchmark interest rate, the risk-free rate will change correspondingly. Because the risk-free rate is a component of the rate of return, that too will change. Changes in specific economic indicators can have a disproportionate impact on certain sectors. Thus, a drop in oil prices is likely to hurt suppliers to the oil industry, but give a boost to businesses with significant fuel costs, such as delivery services.

All of the business and economic factors above influence the selection of an appropriate rate of return. There is, however, no magic formula that sets out rates of returns for specific businesses or sectors. As we noted at the outset, valuation is as much an art as a science. The science is in the formulas and methods; the art is choosing which ones to use. The bottom line is that there is no easy answer.

Choosing a rate of return

A recent search of online and print resources for appropriate rates of return for small businesses reveals little in the way of hard numbers. Given that no two businesses are the same, it's no surprise that most experts would be hard-pressed to generalize. However, the following range of rates of return for small businesses, as quoted by various industry professionals, provides some guidance. As you can see, even the experts have different views.

- A minimum of 25%
- Somewhere between 33% and 100%
- Most small businesses – 29% to 67%
- Smaller companies – 20% to 33%

- Smaller companies dependent on the owner or on a few customers – 25% to 33%
- Most small businesses – 20% to 50%; the vast majority closer to 33% to 50%
- Small to mid-sized businesses with growth potential – 20% to 30%
- Small retail or service businesses with limited growth potential – 30% to 50%
- Consulting businesses, professional practices and one-man businesses – 100%
- Businesses in a growth industry, more than three years in business, exclusive territory, or unique factor – 33%
- Startups with no tangible assets and no access to bank financing – 30% to 40%
- Service businesses dependent on a small number of employees, for example, consulting firms – 33% to 50%
- Manufacturers with annual sales of $1 million to $5 million – 25% to 33%

The rates above range from 20 percent to 100 percent. The simple average is 40 percent, and the most frequently cited rate is 33 percent. By comparison, the 2017 projected return for companies listed on the Toronto Stock Exchange averaged just six percent, according to a Reuters poll. You can see, then, that investors in small businesses demand a significant premium over the risk-free rate, showing once again that investing in a small business comes with considerable risk. Statistics Canada estimates that 28 percent of business startups — or more than one in four — fail in less than two years.

On the other hand, I cannot emphasize often enough that every business is different. The rates above are intended only as a rough guide. Also, bear in mind that if the risk-free rate changes significantly, so will these rates.

Applying the multiple

Blind Ninja

Blind Ninja's blind-installation business has strong growth prospects, but the company needs to hire and train more staff to realize that potential. It currently has just two employees, the owner Bill and Mike, so an expansion of this kind would be uncharted territory. There are no other unusual risks. Using the list as a guide, a rate of return of 50 percent, the high end of the range for a service business dependent on a small number of employees, seems reasonable. If Blind Ninja was not entirely dependent on Bill and Mike, a lower rate of return may have been considered.

The next step is to convert the rate of return to a multiple and apply it to the cash flow. A rate of return of 50 percent equates to a multiple of two (1 ÷ 50% = 2). Multiplying Blind Ninja's expected cash flow of $30,000 (from *Chapter 7*) by two gives us capitalized cash flow, and a value for the business of $60,000.

Blind Ninja

Expected cash flow	$	30,000
Multiple		2 x
Capitalized cash flow	$	60,000

Niche Power

Niche Power is a little more complicated. Its growth prospects as well as those for its industry — power conversion equipment — are moderate. It has a loyal customer base, but 20 percent of its sales come from a single customer. There are no other significant risks. A rate of return of 33 percent seems appropriate, giving a multiple of three (1 ÷ 33% = 3). This rate falls within the range on the list of 25 to 33 percent for manufacturing businesses with annual sales of $1 million to $5 million.

In *Chapter 6* we calculated Niche Power's net assets to be $300,000. If we exclude the land and building valued at $200,000, which we considered to be redundant assets, this leaves us with net assets of only $100,000. Since this is not a substantial amount of saleable assets, a rate of return at the high end of the range is warranted.

Now let's apply the multiple to the cash flows. Niche Power's expected cash flow of $170,000 (from *Chapter 7*) multiplied by three gives us a capitalized cash flow of $510,000.

Niche Power

Expected cash flow	$	170,000
Multiple		3 x
Capitalized cash flow	$	510,000

Business debts and loans

When calculating expected cash flow, we added back interest expense. However, the underlying debts and loans haven't disappeared, and they remain liabilities.

There are two ways to deal with the loans and debts. A buyer could pay the capitalized cash flow amount, but, as part of the deal, require the seller to repay any outstanding debts. Alternatively, a buyer could take over the business with the debt, and pay the seller the net proceeds, in other words, the amount after deducting the debt. Using a house as an example, the value of the business would be akin to the selling price, while the net proceeds would be the amount the selling homeowner receives after paying off the mortgage.

Niche Power's capitalized cash flow as calculated above is $510,000. This amount is also known as the "enterprise value." The company's balance sheet, set out in *Chapter 6*, shows an outstanding bank loan of $20,000. Let's assume that a buyer will keep this debt in the business and pay Joe the net proceeds of $490,000 (the $510,000 less the loan of $20,000) at the time of sale. This $20,000 difference will ultimately be paid when the bank loan comes due. At that time, Niche Power will be under the helm of the new owner.

Niche Power

Capitalized cash flow	$	510,000
Less bank loan	$	(20,000)
Net proceeds to seller	$	490,000

When a loan has been negotiated at less than current market interest rates, a buyer may want to keep the debt in the business, if it is possible to do so. Small business loans are often based on an owner's personal guarantees, and secured against the owner's personal assets in addition to those of the business. In such cases, the lender may require the debt to be repaid when the business is sold.

Business debts may also include advances or loans from the owner. These are typically not kept in the business after a sale. In Niche Power's case, if the $20,000 is an advance from Joe rather than a bank loan, the buyer may agree to pay Joe $510,000 on condition that Joe waives his right to be repaid the advance. Alternatively, instead of waiving being repaid at all, Joe could defer repayment of his $20,000 advance to Niche Power, reducing the buyer's upfront payment to $490,000. In that case, Joe will remain a creditor of the business after the sale.

Blind Ninja has no debts or redundant assets, so the capitalized cash flow of $60,000 is also the value of the business.

Accounts payable and other short-term liabilities are not deducted from capitalized cash flow value, as they are considered part of normal operations rather than debt. The reason is that once they are paid, they are typically replaced by new accounts payable.

Although we have now arrived at a value for Niche Power and Blind Ninja using the capitalized cash flow method, there a few other matters to think about before we're done.

9

Goodwill: Now You See It, Now You Don't

To recap: in *Chapter 8* we arrived at an enterprise value of Niche Power of $510,000. In *Chapter 6* we also determined the current value of net assets at $100,000, excluding the land and building that we considered redundant.

Meanwhile, Blind Ninja was valued at $60,000, with net assets of $50,000. If we subtract the net assets from the value of each business, we can see how much of the total value is "intangible," in other words, not backed by "tangible" or "hard" assets. Tangible assets are those that have a physical existence, such as cash, accounts receivable, inventory, land, buildings, and equipment.

Deducting the net assets from the business value highlights the intangible portion, as shown below.

	Niche Power	**Blind Ninja**
Business value	$ 510,000	$ 60,000
Net assets	$ (100,000)	$ (50,000)
Intangible portion of value	$ 410,000	$ 10,000

A significant amount — 80 percent — of Niche Power's value is intangible. In the case of Blind Ninja, the intangible portion is far lower, at 17 percent.

What's the significance of this intangible value? It is an asset of the business, but it's not one that you can see or touch. In *Chapter 6 — The Asset-based Method*, we mentioned intangible assets such as patents, royalties, licences, copyrights, software, and intellectual property. These types of assets often have a specific legal right of their own and can be sold separately from the business. The intangible value we have calculated here is different because it can't be separated from the business. Rather, it is attributable to the business as a whole — the "magic," so to speak, of the assets, products, services, location, and people that make the business what it is. This is called "goodwill," an accounting term that, unfortunately, does not adequately convey all that it means. Goodwill can be compared to celebrity "star power," that special something that gives famous actors, athletes and musicians an earning ability greater than their net worth.

If goodwill makes up a significant chunk of the business value, as with Niche Power, there are not a lot of hard assets to fall back on should something go wrong. The amount of goodwill can thus affect the risk assessment and the appropriate rate of return. This is why calculating a business's net asset value is important, even when a cash flow method is used. Not only, as mentioned earlier, does it indicate the business's minimum value, but it also allows us to calculate the goodwill portion.

Next we need to consider whether the goodwill is transferable. In other words, will the buyer of the business be able to benefit from it? This is particularly important in the context of a small business. Is the goodwill due to the reputation of the present owner or to the business itself? If the owner's involvement in the business were to end, would the goodwill remain intact? If Bill, the owner of Blind Ninja, stepped back from the business, would the business even survive? If the answer is no, the goodwill is attached to Bill and is not part of the business and cannot be transferred with it. And if goodwill cannot be transferred, it has no value to a buyer. In such circumstances, even when the business is a going concern, an asset-based valuation method would be more appropriate. However, the goodwill may become transferable if the existing owner agrees to stay on after a sale.

Niche Power has a strong management team that can run the business without Joe, and its products have a solid reputation. We'll assume that Niche Power's goodwill stems from the business and not from Joe personally, thus making it transferable to a new owner. As for Blind Ninja, even though it's a two-man shop, the business does have a strong brand beyond Bill. Let's assume that the goodwill in Blind Ninja is also transferable.

If a buyer doesn't want to pay for goodwill, the implication is that there is no value to the business beyond the net assets. It takes time and effort to start a business — securing premises, hiring staff, finding customers, developing infrastructure, and so on. If a buyer is not willing to pay for having all that in place, the alternative is to start a business from scratch, rather than buying an existing one.

It can also go the other way. A young entrepreneur whom I met found a custom manufacturing business that he wanted to buy. He described the owner as "an old-school guy" who started the business from scratch and knew how to make money, but had "run out of steam" and wanted to retire. The entrepreneur is a financially savvy accountant who knows all about goodwill. He saw the business as a going concern. It had a good reputation, earned the owner a decent income, and generated a profit. Surprisingly, the owner was willing to sell for only the value of the equipment and accounts receivable.

"He didn't want anything for goodwill?" I asked, astonished.

"No, he valued his business on assets alone," the entrepreneur replied.

The owner did, however, value the business using his estimate of the market value of equipment, and not what it actually cost him. For example, he had bought $500,000 worth of equipment at an auction for just $300,000. The owner felt he was getting a fair price for the business by asking more than he had paid for the equipment. By the same token, the entrepreneur knew he was getting a good deal by having the goodwill thrown in for free.

Sometimes, a seller might suggest using a cash flow method to value a business, and then add goodwill on top of that. But that would be double counting. The value arrived at with a cash flow method is the entire value of the business, including goodwill.

What if the capitalized cash flow method comes up with an amount less than the value of the net assets? That could be due to a calculation error, or because something has been missed. If not, the business may be a going concern but if the owner can raise more cash by selling the assets than by continuing to operate, the viability of the business is open to question. This could happen when the reason for owning a business is to give the owner a job, and little profit remains after paying his salary. In that case, it may make sense to revert to an asset-based valuation method.

If an amount for goodwill is already recorded on the balance sheet, it dates back to when the existing owner acquired the business. This is because GAAP conservatism only allows goodwill to be recognized on financial statements when an actual transaction takes place. In other words, an owner cannot add some amount for goodwill on to the balance sheet just because the owner believes that it exists. Only in the context of an actual transaction is goodwill considered objective enough to be recorded in the financial statements.

Thus, any existing goodwill on the balance sheet represents the difference between the original purchase price of the business and the identifiable assets at that time. Unless the business was very recently acquired — and that should raise a red flag as to why it is being sold again so soon — the goodwill recorded on the balance sheet could be very different from its current value. The financial health of a business and its value can change quickly. The goodwill on the balance sheet may thus be a far cry from the current value of goodwill, and it should not be included in the net assets calculation. Any existing goodwill will be determined during the current valuation process.

10

Redundant Assets: More Value Apart

Redundant assets, as mentioned in *Chapter 7 — Cash Flow Method*, are those not essential to a business's operations. They may include:

- Equipment or real estate no longer used in operations
- Equipment or real estate that the business could rent or lease instead of owning
- Obsolete inventory
- Surplus vehicles
- Cash or securities in excess of business requirements

If the business you are valuing does not have any redundant assets, you can ignore this chapter. If it does, read on.

Redundant assets can often be extracted from the business and sold separately, potentially boosting proceeds to the seller. Whenever possible, this process should take place prior to the sale of the business, as buyers typically have little interest in assets not needed for operations. If redundant assets remain in the business, the seller may not realize their full value.

Let's use Niche Power as an example of how to deal with redundant assets. The real estate that Niche Power owns is a redundant asset. It is not essential to the business's operations, which could easily be relocated. As mentioned earlier, Joe is considering keeping the property when he sells the business, and leasing it to either the new owner or someone else. He believes that the Toronto real estate market will continue to rise and wants to hang on to a piece of it for a while longer. As well, buyers of his business may prefer to reduce their initial outlay by leasing, rather than buying premises or moving to another location.

Let's see if Joe does realize more by treating the real estate as a redundant asset and separating it from the business. In *Chapter 7* we assumed the property to be redundant and arrived at expected cash flow of $170,000 after adding back $3,000 for property tax as this expense would not be incurred if the property were removed, and deducting $14,000 as the estimated cost to rent alternative premises. If we don't treat the real estate as a redundant asset, then we should not make these adjustments. Let's reverse them. The revised expected cash flow would then be $181,000.

Expected cash flow real estate removed	$	170,000
Property tax adjustment reversed	$	(3,000)
Building rental reversed	$	14,000
Revised cash flow with real estate included	$	181,000

With the real estate included in net assets, there are more tangible assets to support the value of the business. As we learned earlier, a business with more tangible assets, other factors being equal, has less risk. And with less risk, it can command a higher multiple.

Let's assume that if the real estate remains in the business, the multiple will rise from 3 to 3.5. Capitalized cash flow under both scenarios, with and without the real estate, is shown below. When the real estate remains in Niche Power, the capitalized cash flow of the business is higher — $633,500 versus $510,000 without. The increase reflects both the higher cash flow and higher multiple.

Although the value of Niche Power is lower with the real estate removed, this is more than made up by Joe still having possession of the real estate valued at $200,000. The combined value of the business and the real estate is $710,000, compared to $633,500 if he left the real estate in the business.

Niche Power – Redundant Asset Example

Real Estate	Removed	Stays
Expected cash flow	$ 170,000	$ 181,000
Multiple	3 x	3.5 x
Capitalized cash flow	$ 510,000	$ 633,500
Real estate value	$ 200,000	–
Total value	**$ 710,000**	**$ 633,500**

In this example, Joe realizes more by treating the real estate as a redundant asset. That would not be the case however, if the real estate has a lower value, or buyers are willing to pay a multiple higher than 3.5 with the property included. In this simplified example, I've also ignored other factors such as real estate commissions and taxes, which may also affect the analysis.

The important point is that when a business has redundant assets, the seller should consider both scenarios.

11

Discounted Cash Flow: Back from the Future

The capitalized cash flow method that we covered in Chapter 7 assumes a constant cash flow that continues indefinitely. But what if the business's expected cash flows vary so much from year to year that it is not possible to arrive at a meaningful average or constant amount? Or, what if the business is a going concern but has a foreseeable end date? These situations could be due to the following:

- The business has a limited life. For example, it may depend on a single contract to supply product for a fixed number of years, with no assurance of renewal.
- The business has hefty upfront or one-time costs. Many startups incur higher development costs in their early years before generating significant revenue.
- For some businesses the cost of replacing operating assets is significant and varies from year to year, so using an annual average would not paint an accurate picture. A business that replaces expensive equipment every few years, for instance, would probably see big swings in cash flow.
- For businesses with strong growth prospects, expected cash flows

may be much higher in later years. Although we consider growth in choosing a multiple for the capitalized cash flow method, this calculation may not adequately reflect businesses with hockey stick trajectories.

Luckily, there is a valuation method that is ideal in these circumstances — the discounted cash flow method. Let's see how it differs from the capitalized cash flow method, and how to apply it.

Expected cash flow

The calculation of expected cash flow is the same for both methods, with adjustments for non-cash and other items. While the capitalized cash flow method focuses on one year's expected cash flow, and assumes it to continue year after year at the same level, the discounted cash flow method looks at expected cash flow for *each* future year separately, for a specific number of years. While capitalized cash flow uses an annual average for the expected cost of replacing operating assets, discounted cash flow takes into account the amount for each specific year. For a business with a finite life, the discounted cash flow method also includes the likely price for any assets remaining at the end of the business's life, known as their terminal value.

How many years should the discounted cash flow calculation cover? For businesses with finite lives, a reasonable period would be until the cash flows end. For fast-growing businesses, we would normally cover the period until growth levels off. Generally, the range is three to ten years, and commonly five.

The discount rate

With the capitalized cash flow method we multiply one year's cash flow by a number to arrive at a value for the business. However, with the discounted cash flow method no multiplication is needed because we have an estimate of cash flow for *each* future year. What if we simply add up all these future cash flows? Let's look at Elle's forecast of Poker Head's cash flow for the next five years which totals $1.2 million.

Poker Head – Cash Flow Forecast

	Year 1	Year 2	Year 3	Year 4	Year 5	Total
Game Revenue	$ 110,000	$ 300,000	$ 600,000	$ 900,000	$ 1,200,000	
Expenses	$ (100,000)	(250,000)	(400,000)	(560,000)	(600,000)	
Cash Flow	$ 10,000	$ 50,000	$ 200,000	$ 340,000	$ 600,000	$ 1,200,000

Would an investor value Poker Head at $1.2 million? Not likely! Paying $1.2 million and expecting the same amount back over five years amounts to a zero return on investment. Furthermore, there is always a risk that cash flows will not match expectations. In order to earn a return on his or her investment, an investor would need to discount the total cash flow to something less than $1.2 million. How much less depends on the investor's target rate of return. The discount rate thus amounts to the same as the rate of return, and is determined in much the same way.

Why do we call it a discount rate if it's the same thing as a rate of return? It is a standard finance term, and as we are reducing or discounting the cash flows, it accurately describes its purpose.

Let's assume that a discount rate of 40 percent makes sense for Poker Head. Referring to the list of rates suggested in *Chapter 8 — The Multiple*, that's within the 30 to 40 percent range for "startups with no tangible assets and not able to get bank financing."

Applying the discount rate

The next step is to apply the discount rate to the cash flow. It's not as simple as taking the total $1.2 million and discounting that by 40 percent. The "time value of money" needs to be considered, given that the cash flow will come in over a five-year period: $10,000 in one year's time, $50,000 in two, and so on. Receiving cash in the future is not the same as receiving it today. Because money can earn interest, its value increases over time, hence its "time value." Discounting the future cash flow tells us how much it would be worth today. Since we have five different cash flow amounts to be received at five different times, we need to deal with each year separately.

Let's start with Year 1. To discount the cash flow of $10,000 we divide by one (1) plus the discount rate of 40 percent, giving us $7,143.

$$\$10{,}000 \div (1 + 40\%) = \$7{,}143$$

This discounted amount of $7,143 is how much an investor, whose target rate of return is 40 percent, should be willing to pay today to receive $10,000 a year later. As the calculation below shows, if this amount were invested in a one-year term deposit paying a rate of 40 percent (a very unlikely rate) it would indeed grow to $10,000.

$$\$7{,}143 \text{ x } (1 + 40\%) = \$10{,}000$$

In finance terms, the $7,143 is referred to as the "present value." Investopedia defines present value as, "the current worth of a future sum of money or stream of cash flows given a specified rate of return." Using the discounted cash flow method to value a business, therefore, equates to calculating the present value of its stream of cash flows.

Calculating the present value of cash flows beyond the first year is more complicated. Let's look at Year 2. As shown below, dividing the cash flow of $50,000 by one plus the discount rate of 40 percent, gives us $35,714. However, since the cash flow is two years, rather than one year away, the calculation is repeated, using the present value after Year 1, giving us a present value, if received in two years, of $25,510.

Present value if received in one year: $50,000 ÷ (1 + 40%) = $35,714

Present value if received in two years: $35,714 ÷ (1 + 40%) = $25,510

To calculate the present value of Year 3 cash flows, the calculation would be repeated three times. For Year 4, four times, Year 5, fives times and so on. Thankfully, you can find present value calculators online (http://www.investopedia.com/calculator/pvcal.aspx) or in Excel, where you need only plug in the cash flow amount, discount rate, and the number of years (the term). If you're a math whiz, there is a present value formula that you can use. But trust me, using a present value calculator is much easier.

Next we take the present values as calculated for each year's cash flow and add these together. This gives us the discounted cash flow value of the business. The value of Poker Head using this method is $305,605 as shown.

Poker Head

	Year 1	Year 2	Year 3	Year 4	Year 5	Total
Cash Flow	$ 10,000	$ 50,000	$ 200,000	$ 340,000	$ 600,000	1,200,000
Discount Rate	40%	40%	40%	40%	40%	
Term (years)	1	2	3	4	5	
Present Value	$ 7,143	$ 25,510	$ 72,886	$ 88,505	$ 111,561	$ 305,605

As you can see, the present value of the total $1.2 million of cash flows, at a discount rate of 40 percent, works out to just over $300,000. Notice that the further into the future cash flows are extended, the less impact they have on the total value. Thus, the present value of Year 5 cash flow of $600,000 is less than $112,000.

The present value of the cash flows is not necessarily the amount that the seller will receive for the business. As with the capitalized cash flow method, we must deduct debt, and add the value of redundant assets, if any. Poker Head has neither; therefore, its value, as determined above, is a bit more than $300,000. Elle believes that Poker Head is worth this amount. We'll see later if investors agree.

The downside of looking at cash flows several years into the future is that we need to make more assumptions; revenue growth rates, future costs, and so on. For a business such as Poker Head, which has not yet made any sales, let alone a finished product, this means taking a big leap into the unknown. The detailed forecast for Poker Head may give it the appearance of substance and credibility, but Elle could just as well have pulled the $300,000 figure out of thin air.

Many experts consider discounted cash flow to be the most theoretically sound method of business valuation. Its big drawback is that it is complicated. For a business with a constant cash flow, the capitalized cash flow method produces roughly the same result as discounted cash flow, and is much easier to calculate.

12

Early-stage Intangible Assets: The Difficult One

Elle's business is at a much earlier stage than Joe's or Mike's. Poker Head may be more than just an idea, but it is not yet an operating business. Although the game has generated some buzz in the online gaming community, there is a considerable amount of work to be done before it is market ready. After spending $25,000 to develop the demo, Elle's savings are exhausted and she needs more capital to move Poker Head forward.

How would investors value Poker Head? Without any revenues and with insufficient resources to continue, it doesn't meet the criteria of a going concern. As we learned earlier, if a business is not a going concern, an asset-based valuation method is typically appropriate. Yet Elle's business has no tangible or physical assets apart from a computer — not much to value there. But it does have a potentially valuable intangible asset in the form of the brand name, the art, and the code — collectively, the intellectual property — that make up the Poker Head game.

According to the Canada Business Network, "intellectual property is the legal right to ideas, inventions and creations in the industrial, scientific, literary and artistic fields. It also covers symbols, names, images, designs and models used in business." Intellectual property is often legally protected by a copyright, trademark, or patent to prevent others from using it. Other intangible assets — such as software processes, industrial designs, trade secrets, customer lists, computer code and other proprietary technology — may not be legally protected, either because they cannot be, or because the owner has not gone to the trouble and expense of protecting them. Instead, a developer of intellectual property may focus on being first out the gate, hoping that the time and cost involved in developing a similar product will deter others. In the case of Poker Head, Elle and Cole own the copyright together, and have applied to trademark the name.

When a business is a going concern, it may be difficult to determine the value of intangible assets separately from the goodwill. Although Niche Power, as a manufacturer and distributor, likely has some intellectual property in its designs, customer lists and know-how, a prospective buyer is unlikely to acquire them without the rest of the business. We therefore consider them as part of the goodwill. But an intangible asset may have value of its own if it can be extracted and sold separately from the business, and if someone wants to buy it.

The cost method

Businesses based on early-stage intangible assets are notoriously difficult to value. One of my coffee buddies and his business partner developed a device to speed up airport security. They tested a prototype, arranged manufacturing on a contract basis, and were seeking funding for marketing and production. A potential investor suggested a value for the business based on how much money my friend and his partner had put into it. My friend's response, quite correctly, was: "The amount we've spent doesn't reflect the value of our business. We've been frugal with costs and haven't even paid ourselves full salaries."

Even if they had been less cost-conscious, the amount spent would be the replacement cost, in other words, how much someone would need to spend to get to the same stage. As we learned earlier, cost is not the same as value. If a business has revenue potential, and is on the cusp of an avalanche of sales, it is likely to be worth a lot more than the money spent to get there. Conversely, a business with a product that becomes technologically obsolete before its launch probably has little or no value, regardless of the amount spent.

Even so, the cost method is sometimes used to value intangible assets. Elle and Cole arranged a meeting with Richard, the investor who had contacted them through Reddit. Richard is an "angel" investor, in other words, an individual willing to invest his or her own money in early-stage companies. He has invested previously in a number of technology startups, but has no experience developing video games. Richard has offered to put up $80,000 in exchange for a 40 percent stake in a new company that they would incorporate together, and into which Elle would transfer the Poker Head video game. Because Elle has already agreed to give Cole 10 percent of her interest in Poker Head, the remaining 60 percent of the company not owned by Richard would be split 90:10 between Elle and Cole, giving each respectively 54 percent and 6 percent.

Agreeing to invest $80,000 for a 40 percent stake in Poker Head implies a total value for the new company of $200,000 ($80,000 ÷ 40%). How did Richard come up with this number? After Richard's investment, Poker Head would consist of $80,000 cash and the video game. The value attributed to the video game, therefore, is $120,000. If Richard were to justify the value on a cost basis, this would include the $25,000 in costs that Elle paid, with the remaining $95,000 the value attributed to Elle's time during the two years she spent developing Poker Head.

Poker Head		
Cash from Richard		$ 80,000
Value attributed to video game:		
Costs incurred by Elle	$ 25,000	
Value of Elle's time	$ 95,000	$ 120,000
Poker Head implied value		$ 200,000

Discounted cash flow method

How do we reconcile the $300,000 value for Poker Head, as determined by Elle on a discounted cash flow basis in *Chapter 11*, with Richard's valuation of $200,000? Different methods can deliver very different results. If the revenue from an early-stage intangible asset is reasonably predictable, a discounted cash flow method may be appropriate. Richard does not consider this to be the case for Poker Head. The video game has not yet launched, and there are no historical results to support Elle's revenue numbers. She did try to find sales figures for educational video games, but without success. Instead, she based her revenue forecast on a sports-themed video game that had a similar number of demo viewers, a rather tenuous comparison. The problem with forecasts not grounded in actual results is that you may end up with no more than "pie in the sky." Experienced investors like Richard are savvy enough to know that.

As well, Elle's discounted cash flow valuation assumes that Poker Head will have the $100,000 needed to complete the game development, plus funds for marketing and distribution. The cash flow forecast reflects Elle's view of Poker Head's potential, and that can be useful for presentations to potential investors. However, a valuation is based on a company's situation at a specific point in time. The value of Poker Head before Richard's investment and the marketing funding is not the same as it will be after those cash infusions.

Now consider the investment from Richard's perspective. As soon as he puts $80,000 into a company in which he owns 40 percent, he forfeits his right to get back his full investment, barring an agreement to the contrary. For example, if Poker Head has not yet spent the $80,000, and someone else comes out with a similar game, Poker Head may no longer be a viable business. Richard's share of the cash, were the company to be wound up, would be diluted to $32,000 (40% of the $80,000). He would have lost $48,000! After Elle considered the risk Richard was taking, and mindful that he was attributing value to the time and money she had invested in Poker Head thus far, she realized that his offer was quite fair.

The First Chicago method

A more complicated variant of discounted cash flow is the First Chicago method, named after the venture-capital firm that pioneered its use. Developed specifically for early-stage businesses, this valuation method tries to overcome the speculative nature of cash flow forecasts for businesses with no revenue or cost history.

The First Chicago method relies on three cash flow projections: best case, worst case, and expected case. The present value of each scenario is calculated in the same way as the discounted cash flow method. Let's assume that the present value of the best-case scenario is $600,000; worst case, a loss of $300,000; and expected case, $300,000 as determined earlier by Elle.

Each of the three present values is then assigned a probability of occurring — for example; best case 30 percent; worst case 30 percent, and expected case 40 percent. The respective probabilities must total 100 percent. To arrive at a value for the business, we multiply the present value of each scenario by its probability. Thus, the First Chicago method would put Poker Head's value at $210,000.

First Chicago Method

Scenario	Present Value		Probability	
Best case	$ 600,000	x	30%	$ 180,000
Worst case	$ (300,000)	x	30%	$ (90,000)
Expected case	$ 300,000	x	40%	$ 120,000
Value				**$ 210,000**

The First Chicago method addresses the speculative nature of one set of cash flow projections by considering the possibility of others. In Poker Head's case, these scenarios, as well as the assignment of probabilities, are not grounded in historical results. However, taking other outcomes into account probably results in a more realistic value than the $300,000 that Elle came up with. It's worth noting that the First Chicago method arrives at a number much closer to Richard's valuation of $200,000.

The Berkus method

Another way of valuing early-stage businesses is named after Dave Berkus, an American angel investor. Rather than relying on the entrepreneur's revenue and profit projections, Berkus assigns values to what he sees as the various critical elements of a startup. His method addresses what he considers a universal truth, namely, that "fewer than one in a thousand startups meet or exceed their projected revenues in the periods planned." This method's core elements and the value assigned to each are shown below.

Berkus Method

If exists:	Add to company value up to:
Sound idea *(basic value)*	$ .5 million
Prototype *(reducing technology risk)*	$ .5 million
Quality management team *(reducing execution risk)*	$ .5 million
Strategic relationships *(reducing market risk)*	$ .5 million
Product rollout or sales *(reducing execution risk)*	$ .5 million

In his book *The Berkus Method — Valuing an Early-stage Investment*, Berkus explains: "These numbers are maximums that can be 'earned' to form a valuation, allowing for a pre-revenue valuation of up to $2 million (or a post-rollout value of up to $2.5 million), but certainly also allowing the investor to put much lower values into each test, resulting in valuations well below that amount."

The advantage of the Berkus method is that it is easy to apply and focuses on critical milestones in the startup process. In Canada, where investments are usually smaller than in the US, using amounts well below $500,000 for each test may be more realistic. Assuming that Poker Head meets the first test of having a sound idea, but recognizing that its demo is not yet a fully functioning prototype, the Berkus method would put a value of $500,000 on the company. But a more reasonable value, given the stage of Poker Head's development, would probably be half that amount, at most.

Market method

As we learned in *Chapter 3*, the problem with using the market method — finding a comparable business and seeing what it sold for — is finding that suitable comparable. The same applies to an early-stage intangible asset business. Often an idea is worth pursuing because there is nothing else like it. After entrepreneurs exhaust their own funds, the first investment in early-stage businesses — "seed capital," as it is known — often takes the form of "love money" from friends and family. These benefactors often don't even ask for a valuation of the business.

Angel investors, such as Richard, also invest during the seed-capital stage. According to the National Angel Capital Organization's 2015 *Report on Angel Investing Activity in Canada*, members who responded to a survey received close to 4,500 applications from entrepreneurs, sat through over 1,100 presentations, and ultimately funded 25 percent of them. But these transactions are almost always private, and any comparable data that could be gleaned from them is not readily available.

Funding for small businesses also comes from venture-capital firms, which are professionally managed public or private entities that invest in new ventures with high growth prospects. Some venture capitalists invest at the seed-capital stage, but most wait until they can see that the business has potential to grow into something much larger.

Venture capitalists and angel investors often have access to data that they can use to value a target business. They may also rely on information gained through word of mouth and private research, rather than public sources. Again, this information is generally not available to outsiders.

Business incubators

If you are willing to make very broad comparisons — between any technology startup, for example — it may be helpful to look at how specialized investors approach valuations. Business incubators, which provide seed capital and nurture aspiring entrepreneurs through the early stages of business development, typically focus on startups, primarily in the technology sector. But competition for these programs is fierce, with thousands of applicants and only 1.5 to 2.5 percent accepted.[2]

Incubators typically provide the same amount of capital, on the same terms, to each successful applicant, regardless of differences in the companies' business models. My survey of private Canadian incubators — those not linked to a university or specific geographical region — found that they typically offer from $50,000 to $100,000 in exchange for a five to seven percent equity stake in the startup company. This implies a total value for

---

2 Liisa Atva, *Huffington Post* blog, November 2015 — Sowing the Seeds of Startups.

each business of $1 million to $2 million. Should we accept this as a very rough measure of value for those one or two ideas out of a hundred that meet the incubator's acceptance criteria? If so, given the low acceptance rates, such figures would be at the high end and reflect a very optimistic view of these businesses' prospects.

Some incubators give very little weight to cash flow forecasts and business plans. According to one incubator's earlier website, "Business plans are old news in our world... Just fill out the online application — that's all we need! In fact, don't send your business plan even if you've got one." Investors in early-stage businesses tend to rely more on their instincts and experience than on quantitative methods. Only as the business matures and financial information becomes available do cash flow valuation methods become useful.

What these incubators are investing in most of all are people, using intuition as much as hard data. "We take a lot of care in choosing the smartest and most resourceful, dedicated, and passionate people we can find," FounderFuel says. Trevor Blackwell of Y Combinator told a group from SFU's Beedie School of Business, "Succeeding in a startup is, in the most literal sense, extraordinary, so we're looking for people able to do extraordinary things."

When a business has no financial history and an unproven product, it is the founder's ability to build the business that is crucial. "Do the founders seem like people who could build a massive company?" asks Founder Fuel. This means that the value of an early-stage business depends largely on the people involved — a component of that intangible magic that we described earlier as goodwill.

Remember though, goodwill must be transferable if it is to have value; it cannot be tied inextricably to individuals who can leave the business at any time. The further along a product is in its development, the easier it becomes to separate its value from the reputation of the founder or inventor. Thus, Poker Head has more value now that it has completed the artwork and code, than it would if these crucial elements were still all in Elle's head.

Dragons' Den

Where else might we find examples of early-stage, intangible-asset businesses and how they are valued? Perhaps from CBC's Dragons' Den, one of Canada's favourite television reality shows. Applying to appear on Dragons' Den is an easy online process. Getting accepted is not. As Rick Spence reported in the *Financial Post* in 2014, "Producer Richard Maerov, a six-year veteran of the show, expects they'll audition 3,000 people this year for just 250 slots on camera." And only about one in three of those who appear on the show receive an offer from a Dragon, according to Brenda Bouw in the *Globe and Mail* in October 2015. By studying the successful pitches, we can perhaps gain some insights into how savvy and experienced investors, such as the Dragons, value businesses.

The online application includes numerous questions. Those most relevant to valuations, and which often draw attention from the Dragons, include the following:

- At what stage is your business?
- Do you have a patent?
- How much money has been invested in your business so far? (Not including sweat equity)
- How does your business or product make money? Where does your revenue come from?
- What are your sales so far, if any? If possible, indicate sales and profits in dollar amounts or units sold.

I analyzed the successful pitches of early-stage, intangible-asset businesses from several past seasons of Dragons' Den. Most had limited sales, if any, when they appeared on the show. Almost all provided first-year revenue forecasts. About half offered information on expected gross profit. Only a handful gave net income projections.

The value of the business was determined by how much the Dragon offered to invest, and the percentage to be acquired. For example, if the offer was $200,000 for a 20 percent interest, the implied value for the business was $1 million ($200,000 ÷ 20%). Note that this is the amount the business would be worth *after* the investment from the Dragon. As we saw with the value of Poker Head and Richard's proposed investment, the amount invested often makes up a hefty portion of the post-investment value.

The only statistic that I could reasonably infer from the pitches analyzed was the revenue multiple: the business's implied value divided by the first year's expected revenue. On this basis, revenue multiples averaged 1.5 times the first year's expected revenue, with most falling between one and two times. Keep in mind that deals offered by the Dragons during the show can — and often do — change after due diligence and further negotiation. As discussed in *Chapter 4*, rules-of-thumb valuation methods, including revenue multiples, have serious limitations. However, we often have little else to fall back on in the valuation of early-stage businesses.

To repeat, valuing early-stage, intangible-asset businesses is notoriously difficult for a number of reasons: cash flow forecasts that are not based on historical results, a lack of comparables, and a dearth of hard assets. The methods used for other types of small business — net assets and cash flow based — are typically not applicable. As a result, investors may resort to rules of thumb, or even cost-based methods, despite their shortcomings.

In the absence of actual sales, any quantifiable measures are better than nothing. Data on website visits, demo downloads, market size or competitors' performance are all worth capturing. Ultimately, it comes down to what a buyer or investor is willing to pay. The give-and-take of negotiation can also play a role. In Poker Head's case, whether or not Elle agreed with Richard's valuation is irrelevant. She believed that without his investment, her venture would be dead.

13

Structuring the Deal: It's About More than Numbers

Once a price for a business is agreed on, the structure of the deal can have an impact on how much the seller will ultimately receive. By structure, I mean the specific terms that determine how the business will legally be transferred from the seller to the buyer, including any conditions of sale. Here are a few important considerations.

Share or asset sale

A small business is typically either incorporated — in other words, set up as a separate legal entity from the owner — or set up as a sole proprietorship or partnership. When a business is a sole proprietorship or partnership, the assets are owned personally by the proprietor or jointly by the partners. Niche Power is an incorporated company, while Blind Ninja is a sole proprietorship with its assets being Bill's personal property. Elle owns the intangible asset Poker Head although, with no operations yet to speak of, I would hesitate to call it a proprietorship.

The sale of an incorporated business can be structured either as a sale of its assets or its shares. In a sale of assets, the buyer receives a basket of assets, including goodwill, if any. The buyer may also agree to assume specific liabilities of the business, such as accounts payable. The seller would still own the shares of the company, but with the sold assets and liabilities removed. The buyer would only be responsible for liabilities and debts specifically included in the sale. Any liabilities left in the company would remain the responsibility of the seller.

In a sale of shares, the buyer receives the shares of the company, thereby taking over all the company's assets and liabilities. Barring any agreements to the contrary, with a sale of shares employees, contracts, leases and other rights remain with the company to the benefit of the buyer. In an asset sale, these rights can be assigned to the buyer, but that requires the approval of relevant parties such as the employees or lessors, opening up the possibility that they might want to renegotiate the terms of their contracts or other arrangements. Once the shares of a business are sold, the seller no longer has any interest in the company, assuming the sale involves 100 percent of the shares. The sale of a sole proprietorship or partnership is always structured as a sale of assets, since there are no shares.

Owners of incorporated companies typically prefer to sell shares rather than assets. There may be income tax advantages in doing so. Sales of shares are treated as capital gains, which are taxed at a lower rate than other income. As well, if the shares meet the CRA's requirements of a Qualified Small Business Corporation, capital gains up to $835,714 (for 2017 and indexed for inflation thereafter) are exempt from tax.

Buyers, on the other hand, generally prefer to buy assets, as this eliminates the risk of assuming undisclosed liabilities. What's more, the assets of the purchased business may have a higher value than their "taxable" amount, which is the original cost to the seller, less any amounts previously deducted for tax purposes. The buyer records the assets at their current value. The step-up in the cost base of the assets acquired — the difference between the amount paid by the buyer and the amount recorded in the seller's financial records — would result in higher future tax deductions than if the buyer had purchased shares.

When goodwill is included in a deal structured as a sale of assets, it is ascribed a value: the difference between the total purchase price of the business and identifiable assets. The purchased goodwill is subsequently recorded in the buyer's balance sheet at this amount, and will generate future tax deductions for the buyer as an amortization of "eligible capital property."

However, goodwill that is created over time as a business grows does not appear as an asset on the seller's company balance sheet. As mentioned in *Chapter 9 — Goodwill*, the accounting principle of conservatism precludes recording goodwill created internally, as there can be no proof of its value until the business changes hands. And if it hasn't been recorded, it can't be deducted. As a result, the buyer of a business structured as a sale of shares will not get the benefit of future tax deductions in respect of goodwill.

For all these reasons, a buyer may be willing to pay more in a deal structured as assets rather than shares. Of course, there are always exceptions to the rule. Tax losses, mentioned in *Chapter 6*, can only be used in a sale of shares. Since an in-depth discussion of tax issues is beyond the scope of this book, you should consult a tax expert if you are considering buying a company for its tax losses.

Turning again to our three entrepreneurs.... Joe plans to structure the sale of Niche Power as a sale of shares so that he can take advantage of the capital gains tax exemption for Qualified Small Business Corporations. Bill will transfer the assets he uses in Blind Ninja to a newly incorporated company, and then sell 50 percent of that company's shares to Mike. Finally,

Elle will sell her asset — the intellectual property comprising Poker Head — to a new company that she will own jointly with Richard and Cole.

Holdbacks and earn-outs

How and when the purchase price is paid can have a significant impact on the value of a business. A common scenario is for buyers to ask for a holdback, allowing them to pay a portion of the agreed sales price at a future date, rather than when the deal closes. From the buyer's perspective, the less paid up front, the lower the risk of loss in the event that the business does not achieve expected cash flow. For example, a buyer may be willing to pay cash up to the net asset value, with a holdback for the goodwill portion, to be paid over time.

On the other side of the coin, as we learned earlier, a dollar tomorrow is not the same as a dollar today. Even if the holdback is due soon after the sale, the seller always faces some risk that it will not be paid. The seller is effectively lending the amount of the holdback to the buyer. The holdback can be structured as an interest-bearing loan due to the seller, ideally at a rate higher than a bank loan, thereby encouraging the buyer to give priority to paying the seller.

Purchases of small businesses are often financed, in part, from the cash flow of the business after the sale. However, if the buyer pays little cash up front, that means the seller is to some extent being paid with his own money. The seller, therefore, will want the up-front payment to be high enough to discourage the buyer from walking away. In other words, the buyer would need to have "some skin in the game."

A holdback can also be structured as a so-called "earn-out," with the deferred portion of the payment based on future profits. An earn-out is often used to reconcile differences in opinion between buyer and seller on the value of the business. Thus, the parties may agree that the buyer will pay upfront what he or she believes the business is worth, and that the difference between the buyer's valuation and the seller's presumably higher one will be paid as an earn-out. Buyers also use holdbacks as a safeguard against liabilities that may come to light after the sale, or the outcome of a lawsuit that has not yet been settled.

A concern for the seller is that he or she may have little control over an earn-out once the business is sold. A buyer could, for example, incur development costs for new products that push down profits rather than generating cash to settle the earn-out. The terms of an earn-out should be carefully defined. A holdback of between five and 15 percent of the sales price is common, but varies depending on the buyer's reason for wanting one. The length of the holdback period will also depend on the reason; a year or two is not uncommon.

Holdbacks by their nature come with some risk of non-payment to the seller. It is thus quite reasonable for a seller to ask for security for the holdback amount, often in the form of the shares or assets of the business being sold.

Management contracts

If the seller has expertise essential to the business, the buyer may ask him or her to stay on for a while to smooth the transition. If the buyer has no other way to acquire that expertise, he or she may even be willing to pay a higher price for the business in return for the seller signing a management contract for a specified transition period. It may also be worthwhile for the seller to agree to a management contract if the sale includes an earn-out component. If the seller remains involved in the business, he or she will probably be in a better position to ensure that the earn-out is paid.

A client of a business valuator whom I know was looking to sell his business for $5 million. A prospective buyer offered $4.5 million, plus a five-year management contract at a salary of $200,000 a year for a total salary of $1 million. Which was the better deal? If the client took the offer, he would receive $5.5 million in total, half a million more than he wanted as a straight purchase price. But that would also have meant working for another five years. If the seller was planning to retire after the sale, he might understandably be less than thrilled with the offer. On the other hand, he might be happy to accept it if he enjoyed his work and didn't mind staying on. This particular business valuator advises clients to negotiate the sale of their businesses with both these scenarios in mind. They should be ready with a price that includes a management contract for the seller, as well as a "stand alone" deal where the seller severs his involvement with the business.

A buyer may also insist that the deal include "non-compete" and "non-solicitation" provisions. These preclude the seller from setting up a new, competing business or going to work for a rival company and then enticing customers or employees away from the sold business.

How have Joe, Mike and Elle navigated these issues? Joe is willing to enter into a management agreement to stay with Niche Power for up to a year. He will also agree to normal non-compete and non-solicitation terms. If Mike buys a 50 percent stake in Blind Ninja, Bill will agree to remain an acting manager. Because Bill is such an integral part of the business, it may be wise for Mike to ask Bill to sign a management contract. As for Poker Head, Richard, the investor, has already indicated that he wants to cement Elle's role with a management agreement.

Working-capital adjustment

Current assets include cash, accounts receivable, inventory and any other assets that, in the normal course of business, will be converted into cash within a year. Current liabilities include accounts payable and other amounts owing that are likely to be settled within the year. If we subtract the current liabilities from the current assets, we have the "working capital" of a business, in other words, the funds available to a business in the short term.

Working capital is positive when current assets are greater than current liabilities. Generally, a business with positive working capital has sufficient funds to meet its short-term obligations, and it can continue to operate. Working capital can fluctuate over the year, particularly in seasonal businesses. A Christmas-tree farm's working capital, for example, is likely to be negative leading up to Christmas, reflecting almost a year's expenses without sales, but positive after Christmas, its peak sales season.

A business needs a minimum amount of working capital to operate, and to achieve its expected cash flow. Thus, the terms of a sale may require the business to have a specified amount of working capital on hand at the closing date. The amount is usually determined based on what is typical for the business at that time of year, and as negotiated between buyer and seller. If the working capital is more than the specified amount at the closing date, the seller can typically remove the surplus cash from the business. That in effect increases the proceeds to the seller. However, if working capital is less than the specified amount, the shortfall is deducted reducing the proceeds to the seller. These arrangements apply only when the sale of the business is structured as a sale of shares.

We have seen in this chapter that the structure of the sale can have a significant impact on how much the seller receives. Keep in mind when negotiating a sale that the terms of the deal can be as important as the sale price.

14

Partial Interests: When the Sum of the Parts Doesn't Make a Whole

If you're selling or buying 100 percent of a company, you can skip this chapter and the complexities it introduces. However, if only a partial interest is in play, as is the case with Mike and Elle's ventures, read on.

Mike is considering buying 50 percent of Blind Ninja. After Elle transfers the rights to her video game to the new company, to be called Poker Head Ltd., Richard will own 40 percent. Because Elle agreed earlier to give Cole 10 percent of her stake in the venture, she will end up with 54 percent (90 percent of the 60 percent retained), and Cole will own the remaining six percent.

It's important to note that the value of a partial interest in a company is not necessarily the pro-rata value of 100 percent. In other words, if 100 percent of the newly formed Poker Head Ltd. is valued at $200,000, Cole's six percent shareholding is not necessarily worth six percent of $200,000, i.e. $12,000. Why would that be?

Companies are under the direction of and controlled by their shareholders.

If there are multiple shareholders, control lies with the one who holds enough voting shares to outvote the others. If there are two shareholders, Party A with 51 percent and Party B with 49 percent, Party A has control. The more shareholders there are, the more complicated the question of control can be. If Party A and Party B each hold 30 percent and Party C holds 40 percent, Party C has effective control, unless A and B collaborate to outvote C. All shareholdings that are not the controlling interest are considered minority interests.

A company's articles of incorporation, bylaws, and shareholder agreements set out the rights of shareholders, including those of the minority interests. Unless otherwise stipulated, a minority shareholder cannot direct business operations or strategy, sell the business, or decide when to withdraw money from it. Minority interests in a private company may also be more difficult to sell. A buyer of a small business typically wants to be actively involved in running the business, but the purchase of a minority interest may not offer that opportunity or, indeed, the opportunity to wield much influence at all.

Applying a discount to the pro-rata value of the company takes into account the lack of control and the potential difficulty of selling a minority interest. The size of the discount typically ranges from just a few to as much as 40 percent of pro-rata value, depending on circumstances. Factors to consider when determining a discount include the size of the minority interest, the "rules" under which the company operates, as set out in its articles, bylaws and shareholder agreements, and the pool of potential buyers for the shares.

Generally the larger the minority stake, the lower the discount, on the assumption that a larger interest may be able to exert more influence. Securities laws in some jurisdictions allow a sizeable minority shareholder (usually 33.33 percent, but as low as 25 percent in some) to block certain changes that the controlling shareholder may wish to make.

If Mike buys 50 percent of Blind Ninja, both he and Bill would be considered minority shareholders, because neither has control. But because they have equal rights, a discount would generally not be appropriate. By contrast, even a relatively small interest can sometimes be a strategic one. If Party A and Party B each have a 49 percent stake, the owner of the remaining two percent is in a strong position to influence decisions, and may even be able to command a premium for his or her shares.

Minority interests can have a "nuisance value" that negates any discount. Remember when Joe tried to buy out his three original partners in Niche Power? Two of them willingly gave up their 20 percent stakes for the $1,000 they had invested. The accountant, however, held out for $6,000. Niche Power had no sales at that time and its future prospects were uncertain, so it would be hard to argue that the value of the shares had soared six-fold. But instead of engaging in a potentially costly exercise to prove otherwise, Joe paid the accountant's price. He avoided the "nuisance" of having the accountant involved in the future of the business.

Controlling shareholders can't be absolute dictators since minority shareholders have some legal protection, as set out in federal or provincial business corporation statutes or common law. Minority shareholders who have been treated unfairly can apply to the courts for an "oppression remedy." These remedies vary across the country, but they can include requiring the company to buy out minorities at a fair price, or fixing the situation that caused their discontent.

A company's shareholders may agree to different terms from those provided for in the bylaws and corporate statutes. These are typically spelled out in a separate shareholder agreement. In some instances, shareholders may have equal voting rights regardless of the size of their holdings. In that case, a minority discount might not be appropriate. On the other hand, a shareholder agreement may limit when, how and to whom shareholders can sell their holdings, making a minority interest even more difficult to sell. There are many possible permutations of rights and restrictions, but the general rule is that the more rights granted and the fewer restrictions placed on minority shareholders, the lower the minority discount.

In other cases, a shareholder agreement may not grant minority interests special rights, yet still provide that a minority discount should not apply, or that a specific discount rate should be used. It is quite common for a small-business shareholder agreement to include a buy-sell provision known as a "shotgun clause." As the term implies, invoking a shotgun clause is akin to drawing a gun in a standoff. If a shareholder wants out, and a mutually agreeable arrangement cannot be reached, then Shareholder A can give Shareholder B the option of either selling his or her stake at a specified price to A, or of buying A's shares at the same price. A shotgun provision tends to ensure a fair price because the shareholder who offers to buy must also be willing to sell at the specified price. In addition, it provides a mechanism to prevent a prolonged standoff. The existence of a shotgun clause, therefore, reduces a minority discount.

Shareholder agreements sometimes stipulate the valuation method to be used in the event of a purchase or sale. More typically, instead of a valuation method, the agreement states simply that "fair market value" is to be used. This term will be discussed in further detail in *Chapter 15 — Imaginary Sales*, but it best represents the concept of value that we've been striving for throughout this book. Nonetheless, shareholder agreements do not always require fair market value to be used. The valuation method can be anything that shareholders have agreed to, including net book value, net assets, a set formula, or a rule of thumb. I've seen a shareholder agreement stipulate that fair market value must be used, but that goodwill should be excluded. This exclusion would result in a value that is far from fair if the business happens to be a going concern worth more than the value of its net assets.

When a minority interest is for sale, the prospective buyers often include one or more of the existing shareholders, especially if buying the interest would give them control or prevent outsiders from acquiring control. Owners also often encourage trusted employees to buy an equity stake on the grounds that it allows them to take a more active role in the business and to share in the profits. The more potential buyers there are for a minority interest, the lower the discount, if any.

Minority discounts are generally applicable only to private companies. A minority stake in a public company may even trade at a premium to a 100 percent shareholding due to the large pool of potential buyers and the ease and speed at which the shares can be sold.

Selecting a minority discount rate

A range for minority discounts from a few percent to 40 percent is very broad. So how can you determine a more precise number? Given the complexity of the rights and restrictions applicable to minority interests, it may be wise to seek legal advice to fully understand them. Even then, there is no easy answer, and settling on a specific number is ultimately a subjective decision. I have yet to come across any statistics or standard rates on minority-interest discounts that apply to small businesses in Canada.

The list below includes important factors to consider, but there may well be others relevant in certain circumstances. How much weight should you give each factor? Again, there is no easy answer, and each case is different.

Minority Interest Discount

Factors to Consider:	Discount:
The minority interest is 50 percent	No discount
The minority interest would give an acquirer control	No discount
The size of the minority interest	The closer to 50 percent, the lower the discount
Additional rights granted by shareholder agreement	The closer the minority's rights are to the controlling interest, the lower the discount
A shotgun clause in the shareholder agreement	Lower discount
Competition among bidders for a minority interest	Lower discount

Let's use the above list to consider Cole's proposed six percent stake in Poker Head Ltd. His interest is far from a 50 percent interest, and would not give an acquirer control. Therefore, some discount is likely reasonable. Let's assume there is a shareholder agreement that contains a shotgun clause, but grants no extra rights to minority shareholders. Apart from Elle and Richard, Poker Head's two other shareholders, there are no obvious potential buyers. Based on these assumptions, let's assume that a minority discount of 30 percent would be appropriate. Were it not for the shotgun clause, a discount at the high end of the typical range might be reasonable.

Once we've settled on a discount rate for the minority interest, it's a simple matter to apply it. Assuming a value of $200,000 for Poker Head, the pro-rata value of Cole's six percent interest is $12,000. After applying a 30 percent discount, the value of his interest drops to $8,400. As you can see, a minority interest discount can have a significant impact on value.

Pro-rata value Cole's 6% interest	$	12,000
Less: 30% discount	$	3,600
Value of Cole's interest	**$**	**8,400**

A much lower discount, perhaps as low as 10 percent, would be appropriate for Richard's 40 percent interest in Poker Head. A stake of this size is typically large enough to block some actions that a controlling shareholder might try to force through. As well, the shotgun clause likely has more clout.

15

Imaginary Sales: Divorce, Disputes and Reorganizations

Joe, Mike and Elle are all contemplating actual or "open market" transactions in which the selling price of their businesses will be decided through negotiation with parties that are at "arm's length." We use the term arm's length if the parties are not related and have no other connection that may cause them to treat each other more favourably. If Joe sells his company to an arm's-length buyer, he will want to receive the highest price possible. If, instead, he chooses to sell to his son, he may be willing to accept a lower price.

There are times when you may need to determine what a business is worth, even though an open market transaction is not planned. Divorce is one example. When a business is part of the assets subject to a divorce settlement, it needs to be valued. Although the divorcing spouses may have no intention of actually selling the business, a financial settlement between them would be impossible without knowing its value. This process is the same as when one of the divorcing spouses keeps the family home and an appraisal is required in order to buy out the other spouse's interest.

A valuation may also be needed for income-tax purposes in conjunction with company reorganizations, estate planning, or when a business is transferred from a sole proprietorship to a company. Business valuations may also be required for disputes or arbitration between shareholders or other parties. Divorce and reorganizations are the two most common reasons for valuations for imaginary sales. In all these cases, the business is not up for sale, but its value needs to be determined as if it were.

You should seriously consider hiring a court-recognized expert when a business is being valued for a divorce settlement, or any other dispute that may end up in court. More on this in *Chapter 17 — Hiring an Expert.* Let's continue and I'll explain how this type of valuation differs from one leading to an open market transaction, and how we lay the groundwork for a generally accepted definition of "fair market value."

Valuing a business for an imaginary sale — also known as a "hypothetical" or "notional" sale — is similar to the process for an actual transaction. However, we need to make certain assumptions in the absence of an open market in which these factors would arise naturally.

At a point in time

The value of a business being bought or sold is at a specific point in time. All being well, Joe, Mike and Elle will finalize their deals shortly after they complete their negotiations. What is relevant to them is the current value of the business, in other words, what it is worth at that very moment.

With hypothetical sales, the valuation date can be the present or sometime in the past. In divorce proceedings, assets are often valued as of the date of separation, which can be months or even years before the valuation is undertaken. In those situations, the specific date is important because the value of the business can change markedly over time. For example, a taxi licence in Vancouver was reportedly worth $1 million a few years ago. But the trade in licences has all but dried up recently with the uncertainty over Uber's entry into the market.

Valuations as of a current date generally incorporate every known and relevant fact. But with valuations for hypothetical purposes as of a date in the past, hindsight — information that could not reasonably be known at the valuation date — is generally not allowed. For example, if a Vancouver taxi licence were the subject of a valuation for a hypothetical sale with a valuation date before Uber came on the scene, the valuation would not take Uber's impact into account.

Highest price possible

When valuing a business for a hypothetical sale, we assume the highest price possible. In our divorce example, the spouse receiving a payout may prefer a higher value for the business, while the spouse making the payment would like a lower one. Why assume the highest price possible? Because doing so provides a more realistic value. The seller of a business will press for as high a price as possible. Of course, the seller may not get the asking price, but will come down only to the degree that he or she has to and, presumably, only after trying to find another buyer willing to pay the full asking price.

Note that the assumption is the highest price *possible*, not the highest price imaginable. The price must still be realistic. In divorce cases, it is not uncommon for spouses' valuations to differ, sometimes significantly. There is a saying that if you have two values, one of them is bound to be wrong — maybe even both. If the matter goes to court, ideally each valuation is considered on its own merits, and the one that most closely reflects the amount that would be received if the business were sold is chosen. Sometimes, it will be the lower value, sometimes, the higher. A court may also impose its own value somewhere in between.

In order to determine the highest price possible, you should consider buyers who, for various reasons, may be willing to pay more for the business than others. For example, a competitor may be able to achieve cost savings or higher sales by combining the two businesses. We call buyers who may be able to realize benefits that others cannot, "special purchasers." We'll discuss them in further detail in *Chapter 16 — How to Get a Higher Price.*

Open and unrestricted market of buyers

The greater the number of bidders for a business, the higher the price the seller is likely to achieve. For example, if the seller of a property receives multiple offers, chances are that a bidding war will erupt, driving up the price. With a valuation for a hypothetical sale, we assume that no buyers are excluded, and that any restrictions on the sale are temporarily lifted. Thus, if the highest price for a business being valued for divorce purposes would likely come from a competitor, neither party can make the argument that the shareholders would never approve such a sale.

Buyers and sellers are informed and careful

A valuation for a hypothetical sale assumes that the parties involved are informed, careful, and will learn what they need to know about the business. Sellers should not assume that they can take advantage of a buyer's lack of knowledge. In an open market transaction, the seller may allow the buyer to talk to key customers or suppliers. But that is often not the case in a divorce valuation. However, we assume that any information a buyer would glean if they were allowed to talk to others is taken into consideration.

Neither party is under pressure

The seller of a business may, for various reasons, need to move fast in an open market transaction. But with a hypothetical sale valuation, we assume that there is no pressure to act. The business would not be sold as quickly as possible, nor at any cost.

Stated in cash

A valuation for a hypothetical sale assumes an all-cash deal. This simplifies the process by eliminating the need to adjust the value of the business for any structuring elements such as earn-outs, deferred payments, and the other items discussed in *Chapter 13 — Structuring the Deal.*

Definition of "fair market value"

You may have heard the term "fair market value." The definition most commonly used by business valuation experts and generally accepted by the courts is the following:

"The highest price available in an open and unrestricted market between informed and prudent parties, acting at arm's length and under no compulsion to act, expressed in terms of cash."

This definition captures all the assumptions that we discussed in the context of valuations for imaginary sales and is often used in shareholder and other agreements that may impact the value of a business.

16

How to Get a Higher Price

If you're ready to sell your business, how do you get the highest possible price? Understanding how businesses are valued is a good start, and if you've read this far, you hopefully do. Ideally, you started thinking about your "exit plan" years ago, as it can often take time to implement value-enhancing strategies, and reap their benefit.

If you were planning to sell your house, a real estate agent would likely advise you to do a few things to make it more attractive to buyers. For starters, you would want the house to look its best when buyers show up on the doorstep. Things to do might include a general clean up, some painting, any needed repairs and, perhaps, value-adding renovations. Then there's the question of timing. If the real estate market is livelier in the spring or summer, you might do best to wait until then to list your house. Finally, the wider you cast your net — for instance, by having an agent list the house on the Multiple Listing Service (MLS) rather than trying to sell it yourself — the better the chances of attracting buyers, and perhaps even stoking a bidding war. Selling a business is no different.

Readying a business for sale

As we've shown in previous chapters, the higher the expected cash flow and the lower the risk of not attaining it, the higher the value of the business.

It follows that finding ways to improve cash flow and reduce risk should increase value. Think of this as the clean-up, repair and renovation phase. But in weighing your options, keep in mind that the goal is to add value, not simply to recoup money spent. Here are some ideas that may be useful:

- Stay up to date on industry developments; capitalize on the opportunities, and be aware of potential risks.
- Protect intellectual property with patents and copyrights when possible.
- Solidify customer relationships and consider long-term contracts that make revenue more predictable.
- Diversify your sales to reduce dependence on one or a few big customers.
- Diversify key suppliers to reduce the risk of being overly dependent on any one of them.
- Strive to make the owner dispensable so that goodwill is transferable.
- Put strong managers in place, for the same reason.
- Document systems and put in place processes that minimize reliance on specific individuals.
- Resolve any employee issues that threaten the work environment.
- Ensure financial data is current and adequate, including interim financial statements, budgets, forecasts, and detailed lists of assets. "Adequate" does not mean that the financial information should be audited. Most small businesses are not required to have their financial statements audited, and the expense of doing so is often not warranted. Even so, financial statements should be prepared with care and diligence, as potential buyers will scrutinize them. If necessary, update accounting systems and develop metrics that can be monitored.
- Review leases and other contracts to ensure they are easily transferable.
- Push to collect overdue accounts receivable.

- Get rid of obsolete inventory, as buyers will discount it anyway. Keeping it may give the impression that inventory isn't moving, and that the business is out of touch with its market.
- Ensure equipment is in good order and update if necessary.
- Remove redundant assets from the business and sell them separately.
- Install new signage and repaint for a well-taken-care-of look.
- Ensure the business has adequate working capital, as this will make it a more attractive target.
- Reduce unnecessary expenses.
- Exclude non-business expenses. Small business owners may be tempted to channel personal expenses through the business. This not only increases the risk of a tax audit — personal expenses are not allowable business expenses — but also reduces the cash flow of the business.
- Update the business's website, technology, and social media platforms.

It takes time to implement many of these measures and for their impact to show up on the business's financial performance. In particular, finding and grooming the right managers can take a few years. Even if you're not yet ready to sell your business, it's never too early to start thinking about how to enhance its value. Not only are the suggestions above useful for adding value, they are also sound business practice.

Timing the sale

When is the right time to sell a business? As with selling a home, the decision can be an emotional and time-consuming process. Owners should be sure they are committed to selling before seeking out buyers. Putting a business up for sale, perhaps to gauge buyer interest, then not going through with the sale is risky. It may be difficult to convince buyers that you're serious the next time around; in the meantime, the uncertainty could hurt the business.

Even if you've made the decision to sell, and readied the business for sale, you may want to wait before actually putting it on the market. Like real estate, the value of a business is affected by the state of the economy and market conditions. During the credit crisis of 2008, many potential buyers of businesses adopted a wait-and-see attitude. On the other hand, when the economy is strong, buyers may be more optimistic about a business's potential and willing to pay more. By the same token, low interest rates tend to push down targeted rates of return, which may lead to a higher value for a business. But a seller also needs to be realistic. It's not always possible to wait for an ideal time to sell and sometimes the decision is forced by events beyond an owner's control.

Naturally, it makes more sense to sell a business after a good year than after a poor one. Strong cash flow in the past will lend credibility to forecasts of strong cash flow in the future. As well, it may be difficult to convince buyers that a bad year is an anomaly and not the start of a downward trend.

Owners should also keep in mind the number of businesses expected to change hands in the future — potentially 500,000 in the next decade in Canada alone. If a number of similar businesses come on the market at the same time, selling prices may suffer. As business-succession consultant Peter Merrick put it in the Vancouver Sun, "It's going to be a buyer's market so if someone is contemplating getting out, it's like musical chairs — you want to choose your chair early because later on there's going to be a lot of people."

Buyers and special purchasers

The greater the number of interested buyers, the higher the final price is likely to be. However, unlike the MLS for real estate, Canada has no one-stop shop for small business listings. As a result, it may be difficult to bring a business to the attention of all potential buyers. Brokers and other experts involved in selling businesses can be helpful, as discussed in *Chapter 17 — Hiring an Expert.*

Bear in mind that some buyers, for reasons of their own, may be willing to pay more for a business than others. A potential buyer who can envision higher revenues or lower costs or some other strategic benefit, is known as a special purchaser. To the extent possible, a seller should try to identify such special purchasers. One way of doing that is to consider the business's existing relationships:

- Industry associations and active participation in them may bring owners into contact with potential buyers.
- Competitors may be interested in buying the business if they can achieve economies of scale, either by increasing revenue or lowering costs. For example, a competitor may be able to add customers without adding salespeople or distribution channels; obtain access to a specific customer; reduce competition and subsequently raise prices; blend product offerings; or consolidate manufacturing, warehouse or office locations.
- Suppliers may be able to boost revenue by having the target business buy more of their product, or improve its profitability by selling product to it at a lower price. A brewery buying a pub and then turning it into an outlet for its own beer — the producer becoming the retailer — is an example of this vertical integration.
- Customers that already have a need for the products may be able to reduce costs by buying the business.
- Employees may be potential buyers, either individually or as a team. They have the advantage of knowing the business and the people involved, and may wish to secure their future employment, bring

in revenue with their own contacts, or believe that they can operate the business more efficiently than the current owner.

- Potential new entrants to the market may be able to ramp up faster and more easily by buying an existing business rather than starting one from scratch.
- Location hunters may want to buy a business solely for its land and, perhaps, buildings. For example, if the business is located on a lot coveted by a nearby car dealership, the dealership may be willing to pay a premium price that has little to do with the value of the business and everything to do with its location.
- Private equity or venture-capital investors typically look for larger businesses than those covered by this book. But a business with significant growth prospects may catch their eye.

I met the proprietor of a local café who was selling his business. It operated from leased, not owned, premises in a quaint heritage building. A real estate agent, who had sold a number of restaurants in the same neighbourhood, suggested listing the business at $95,000. If the agent had used a cash flow method, as would be appropriate for the going concern that it was, the multiple to arrive at that price would be about 10 times cash flow, equating to a rate of return of 10 percent — a low rate for the risk involved in a small business. I advised the owner to list his café with the agent. If the agent could indeed sell the café for that price, the owner would do very well.

The business had been on the market for a few months when the agent presented the owner with two offers of $45,000. The owner had also mentioned to a few of his regular customers that he was thinking of selling. While he was still considering how to respond to the two offers, one of his customers came through with an offer of $65,000. The customer, who had recently left her marketing position, had fallen in love with the café and had a vision for the business that, with her background, she was confident she could achieve. In other words, she was a special purchaser.

A seller will not necessarily know much about a buyer's motivation, resources, or possible synergies but, to the extent possible, he or she should try to find out what they are. The buyer who is likely to benefit the most from owning the business may be willing to pay more. Sellers should not expect the price to reflect all the benefits to a buyer since there is always a risk that at least some of these benefits will not materialize. The greater the uncertainly in realizing the benefits, the less likely the buyer will be to pay for them.

A seller should also not expect a buyer to pay for the value that the buyer brings to the business. Mike sees potential for Blind Ninja to become a distributor of blinds through his contacts in China, but Blind Ninja should be valued without that extra income that Mike may be able to bring about.

Negotiating

Canadians are likely to buy and sell an average of nine to 12 cars and five or six houses during their lifetimes, but few will buy or sell even a single business. Thus, most have little opportunity to hone the negotiating skills needed for this kind of transaction. While negotiating ability does not affect the value of a business, it can make a real difference to the price. Remember, as Warren Buffet said, "Price is what you pay. Value is what you get." After you've valued the business, timed the sale and identified special purchasers, be careful not to give away that hard work during the negotiation process. With so much at stake, it may be advisable to seek help for the negotiations. We routinely do just that by hiring a real estate agent to help buy or sell our homes, yet business owners often try to do it themselves, even though the business could be worth a lot more than a house or condo.

Having someone negotiate on your behalf can also take much of the emotion out of the process, possibly leading to a better outcome. Business valuation and other experts can help with the negotiating process. More on experts in the next chapter.

Even once you have come up with a reasonable estimate of a business's value, there is no guarantee that it will sell for that amount. Until it is actually put on the market, it's not possible to fully gauge buyers' interest, motivation or negotiating abilities, all of which are likely to have a bearing on the final price.

17

Hiring an Expert

It is possible to value a business yourself — and if you've read this far, you're already much better equipped than most to do so. Nonetheless, there are times when it may be wise to call in an expert. Just because you know the business better than anyone else doesn't mean you're the best person to value it, find buyers, negotiate and structure the deal. A business valuation expert can do all that. Several types of professionals have expertise in this area.

Real estate agents

Browse your local real estate listings and you'll find businesses listed for sale, mostly restaurants, stores and service businesses. If your business includes a building or property, a real estate agent may be indispensable to the sales process. A word of caution: as we've learned, a business is made up of much more than its real estate. If you are considering using an agent to sell your business, make sure he or she has experience valuing businesses. If the agent does but relies predominately on rule-of-thumb valuation methods, that could be to your disadvantage.

Finding a business to buy or finding buyers for an existing enterprise is not easy given that there is no central businesses-for-sale listing service comparable to the real estate MLS. As a result, real estate agents' access to the MLS can be an advantage given the broad exposure that it can provide.

What if you want to sell your business separately from any real estate it owns? As we learned in *Chapter 10*, if the real estate is redundant — that is, not integral to the business operations — you may realize more from the sum of the parts. In that case you'll definitely want to involve a real estate agent for the property, but that doesn't preclude you using a different expert to help sell the business.

Real estate agents typically work on a commission basis with negotiable rates ranging from one to seven percent on the first $100,000, and 3.5 percent on the balance, with the commission paid by the seller only if the sale closes. However, those rates are for property deals. The commission for selling a business is often higher — 10 percent is not uncommon — and there may be a minimum fee.

Typically, real estate agents earn commissions as the listing agent for the seller, without a separate fee for the valuation. For hypothetical transactions, when an actual sale will not take place and no commission will be earned, an agent would have no incentive to provide a valuation, and it would not be reasonable to expect one to do so. In those circumstances a real estate appraiser is typically hired to value the business's real estate, but not the business itself.

Business brokers

Business brokers typically work with small to mid-sized private companies to value businesses, bring together buyers and sellers, and assist in the negotiation and sale process. Many provinces require business brokers to hold a real estate licence. Although their focus may be the business rather than the property, if they hold a real estate licence, they can also handle the real estate components of a sale. Ideally, a business broker has specific training in valuing businesses, although there is no such requirement.

When engaging a business broker, it is advisable to ask about his or her expertise, qualifications and references.

Some business brokers are members of the International Business Brokers Association (IBBA), a non-profit group with a Canadian chapter. The IBBA's primary focus is to promote professional standards through education and training. It offers a Certified Business Intermediary designation with a number of required courses that include analyzing financial statements, pricing small businesses, and ethics and standards. Business brokers in Canada may also be Chartered Business Valuators, another accredited designation, described in detail later in this chapter.

Turning to our three characters, Joe received an email from a US-based business brokerage group offering free valuations. Its subject line was "Sell your business for maximum value." He attended a seminar and ended up being offered a free valuation for Niche Power. But there was a catch. If, after receiving his free valuation, he engaged the group to sell his business, it would charge a minimum fee of $50,000 with no assurance of the price he would receive. Corporate finance expert Axel Christiansen advises: "You see a number of very fancy presentations coming in from the States, but I don't know too many people who have had very good experiences there. You want someone who knows the local market, especially for smaller businesses."

Business brokers may already have rosters of potential buyers for specific kinds of business, or will know how to find them. They can help screen buyers while keeping details of your business confidential. Secrecy can be important. If employees, suppliers or customers learn that a business is for sale, they may leave or take their business elsewhere. Brokers with established networks can expose your business to prospective buyers without alerting vested parties that it is for sale. They can also screen potential buyers to eliminate those that either lack the resources or are not serious in their intentions.

As for fees, according to reporter Jenny Lee in *The Vancouver Sun*, "Those who sell businesses valued under $1 million charge eight to 12 percent of the value of the company; lower mid-market brokers sell $5-million to $100-million companies for four to 10 percent." Business brokers whom I surveyed seem to fall within this range. "I charge 10 percent on the first $1 million and six to seven percent up to about $5 million," one broker told me.

Business brokers need time to learn about your business. Be suspicious if the valuation seems superficial or the broker is too quick to suggest using a rule-of-thumb method. An in-depth valuation takes time. It is reasonable for brokers to ask for a retainer to be credited against the fee earned on the sale of the business, or in addition to it. Retainer fees range from $3,000 to 10 times that amount, and several brokers have told me that their minimum retainer is $10,000. Again, be skeptical of free valuations. They may be offered just to get your business, and may thus come up with unrealistically high values.

Make sure you understand how and when the broker's fee is to be paid. Ideally, you would structure the payment on the same terms and timing as you receive the proceeds from the sale of the business. But broker fees may sometimes be due even if the deal does not close. Such an arrangement may not be unreasonable given the amount of work entailed in valuing a business. You may want a lawyer to review your contract with the broker.

Investment bankers

Investment bankers are more likely to be involved in the sale of public and large private companies valued at $5 million or more. However, some may be interested in assisting startups with promising growth prospects.

Chartered Professional Accountants

The Chartered Professional Accountant (CPA) designation, the pre-eminent accounting qualification in Canada, is respected and recognized globally. CPAs must have a minimum level of competency in financial reporting, strategy, corporate governance, management accounting, auditing, finance and taxation. There are no requirements for proficiency in business valuations. Even so, CPA Canada, the profession's regulatory body, does offer business valuation courses, and many CPAs do have experience in this area.

CPAs may charge for business valuations on an hourly basis, or a fixed fee, or as a percentage of a business's selling price, as do business brokers. The hourly rate generally varies from $250 to $600 or more. Expect to pay at the top end of that range for a CPA with business valuation experience.

Chartered Business Valuators

The Canadian Institute of Chartered Business Valuators is the premier body in Canada for business valuations. The institute sets guidelines, has a code of ethics, and helps develop professional standards, valuation theory, practices, and education. Chartered Business Valuators (CBVs) are specifically trained in business valuations, corporate finance, and litigation support for financial matters. The courts recognize CBVs as experts in cases that involve business valuations, such as family law, shareholder or partnership disputes, and intellectual property disputes, among others.

CBVs have a very specific expertise, and they do not come cheap. Fees may be on an hourly basis, a fixed project fee, or a percentage of a business's selling price. Many CBVs are CPAs as well with comparable or slightly higher rates, typically from $300 to $600 or more an hour. CBVs who work as independent consultants, without the overhead of a large professional practice, may charge at the lower end of the range. The cost of a business valuation can vary, so it's best to talk to several valuators before choosing one. Also, be sure you clearly understand the assumptions and expectations that go into the cost estimate.

The cost of a business valuation will also depend on the type of engagement and report required. The Canadian Institute of Chartered Business Valuators lists three standard types of valuation report which vary in the scope of review, the amount of information disclosed, and the level of assurance provided:

- A **comprehensive** report, the highest level, provides an opinion on the value of shares, assets or an interest in a business based on a thorough review and analysis of the business, its industry, and all other relevant factors. This type of report is typically required when the valuation is for legal proceedings such as divorce cases or other disputes that may end up in court.
- An **estimate** report provides a valuation based on a limited review, analysis, and corroboration of relevant information. This type of report may be used for certain types of hypothetical transactions such as estate planning, or where the transaction may be subject to scrutiny by the Canada Revenue Agency.
- A **calculation** report offers a more limited review and analysis. It provides a rough value of the business, and may be adequate for buying or selling a business, or to complete a shareholder agreement.

Not surprisingly, the comprehensive report is the most costly of the three, and is typically commissioned when there is a prescribed need for one, subject to court or other scrutiny. However, even the simplest calculation report can start from $4,000 to $6,000. Several independent CBVs whom I interviewed said that their average fee was in the range of $15,000 to

$20,000, but added that their clients were more likely to be mid-sized businesses with revenues of $10 to $50 million.

The cost of a full CBV report is beyond many small-business budgets. However, you don't typically need a formal report to give an indication of value when buying and selling a small business. CBVs can also be valuable as advisers to help prepare a business for sale, ideally several years in advance. They are also well equipped to take on the role of broker, bringing buyers and sellers together, and guiding the negotiation and sale process.

The decision to hire an outside valuation expert often boils down to cost versus benefit. Experts are not inexpensive, but a good one may prove to be invaluable.

18

Decision Time: What Did Joe, Mike and Elle Do?

Let's see how our three almost-real characters navigated the decisions they faced. Was Joe able to sell Niche Power for a reasonable price? Did Mike buy into Blind Ninja? Was Elle content with how much of Poker Head she gave up for the funding she needed?

Joe and Niche Power

Joe hired a local business broker, who is also a CBV, to help him with the sale of Niche Power. Prior to listing the company for sale, Joe transferred the land and building from Niche Power to a new company that he will continue to own. Joe wanted to hang on to the real estate and lease it to either the buyer of the business or another tenant. The broker considered Niche Power to be a going concern, and used the capitalized cash flow method to value the business. The broker arrived at a value of $490,000 for Niche Power (the same value used in the example in *Chapter 8* assuming the company keeps the $20,000 bank loan).

Joe received an offer of $500,000 from a competitor for 100 percent of the shares of Niche Power. The offer included a holdback of $100,000 to be paid out over two years, subject to Niche Power meeting various revenue targets. Joe accepted the offer, which included a condition that he stay on for one year at his current salary. He believes that this arrangement was key to getting the price that he did for the business, as the buyer did not have a manager ready to move into the role.

The broker valued the business, found the buyer, structured the sale, and negotiated the selling price for a fee of $40,000, based on eight percent of the selling price. Joe also involved his own accountant, a CPA, to review the tax implications of the sale. He hired a lawyer to draw up the legal agreements to complete the transaction. He will engage a real estate agent later if he decides to sell the land and building.

Mike and Blind Ninja

Mike initially considered investing in a blind-installation franchise, but he opted instead to buy into Blind Ninja. He had several good reasons for doing so: lower up-front costs, an established business, the potential of becoming a supplier of blinds, and the opportunity to work with someone he already knew. Bill, the owner, calculated the value of Blind Ninja himself after reading this book. He concluded that the business was a going concern and used the capitalized cash flow method to arrive at a value of $60,000. He ended up offering Mike a 50 percent stake for $30,000.

After Mike's investment of $30,000, Blind Ninja had net assets of $50,000. A value of $60,000 for Blind Ninja implies goodwill of $10,000. Mike considered this goodwill transferable because it was not solely attributable to Bill's involvement and, in any event, Bill would remain active in the business. Mike agreed that $30,000 was a reasonable price for 50 percent of Blind Ninja, and that a minority discount was not applicable — as a 50 percent shareholder he had the same rights as Bill. Meanwhile, Bill incorporated a new company into which he transferred the assets used in Blind Ninja. Mike paid the $30,000 to the new company, and half its shares were issued to him.

Mike and Bill doubled Blind Ninja's revenues in less than a year, thanks mainly to the planned expansion into Alberta. When business there slowed, they redirected their marketing efforts to British Columbia, and shortly afterwards placed their first order for blinds from China.

Elle and Poker Head

Elle had spent two years, and her savings of $25,000, developing the video game concept for Poker Head. She and Cole joined forces to come up with the proof of concept that they used to gauge interest from the gaming community. Based on the feedback they received, Elle and Cole were confident that the game would be a winner. However, without extra funding, they were unable to continue development work. Luckily for them, Richard, the investor they found through Reddit, offered to put up $80,000 in exchange for 40 percent of a new company that would hold all the rights to the Poker Head video game.

Richard used the cost method to value Poker Head at $200,000. This estimate included his investment of $80,000 cash plus the video game, to which he attributed a value of $120,000. Elle accepted Richard's offer because it recognized her contribution of time and money, and enabled her to continue developing Poker Head. In addition, she had to face the reality that no other offers were on the table. The good news was that within 18 months of Richard's investment, Elle and Cole had a functioning game, and were ready to start exploring marketing and distribution options. The future was looking bright for Poker Head, and for its three shareholders.

Three different businesses, three different perspectives, and a variety of valuation methods. The stories of Joe, Mike and Elle underline a central theme of this book, namely that there is no one-size-fits-all method when it comes to valuing a business, even a small one.

When determining how much a business is worth, the interests of sellers and buyers are often diametrically opposed. One wants to buy at the lowest possible price, the other is determined to sell at the highest. One may see value where the other sees none. They may not agree on future prospects for the overall economy, the sector, and the business itself. In short, a valuation that seems reasonable to one may look wildly unrealistic to the other.

How do we bridge this gap? Sellers need to put themselves in a buyer's shoes and ask some hard questions. Can the business survive without me? In other words, is the goodwill transferable? Are my forecasts reasonable? Are there risks I have not considered? How do I make the business more appealing? Buyers, on the other hand, need to think like investors and not allow emotion to cloud their judgment. What is a reasonable rate of return for the business as is? Will it need additional skills or resources to achieve the targets set?

The bottom line is that if sellers need to think like buyers, and buyers need to think like investors, then everyone needs to think like an investor. And that is precisely the approach that this book takes to valuing a small business — think of the business as an investment.

Let's recap the process of valuing a business. First we considered the market method — finding a comparable business and seeing what it sold for. We concluded that there would likely be few, if any, instances of a comparable sale to justify using this method.

Next we considered rules of thumb. While these are easily applied they not necessarily accurate or reliable for every situation. However, they do play an important role in the valuation of professional practices, when what is being sold is a "book of business" or a client list, rather than a company. As well, a rule of thumb may be useful as a rough estimate of value, or as an extra check on a value determined by other methods.

When we look at a business as an investment, the price an investor is willing to pay depends on how much cash he or she expects to receive from it, and when. To clarify the how and when, we need to determine whether a business is a going concern. If not, its value is tied to how much its assets can be sold for, and an asset-based valuation method is appropriate. For going concerns, we need to look beyond the value of the assets to the cash that the business is likely to generate in the future, which makes a cash flow valuation method more useful.

The ins and outs of the asset-based method were explained, as was the importance of calculating net asset value, even if a cash flow valuation method is ultimately used.

Moving on to cash flow-based methods, we discussed how to determine expected cash flow, how to choose a rate of return and its corresponding multiple, and whether to use the capitalized or discounted cash flow method.

Valuing early-stage, intangible-asset businesses is not quite so easy. We discussed other valuation methods that could be considered.

Since the structure of the deal can have an impact on how much the seller ultimately receives, the following were explained: asset or share sales, deferred payments, earn-outs, management contracts and working capital requirements. How and when a minority interest discount should be applied was also discussed.

Next we introduced the concept of fair market value in the context of imaginary or hypothetical sales. The definition provided is one that is generally accepted in Canadian courts.

Possibly the most important chapter in the entire book is *Chapter 16 — How to Get a Higher Price.* Knowing how businesses are valued can enhance the value of a small business. This chapter provides some strategies to do that.

Lastly, an important consideration: should you hire an outside expert or advisor? Valuing a business is not a simple matter. Even if you have a solid understanding of the process involved, in many circumstances it may be wise to involve an expert.

Whether you're selling, buying, investing in, or still growing a small business, I hope I've helped you answer the important question of how much it's worth.

19

List of Words: A Handy Reference

Accrual accounting: An accounting method in which sales and/or revenue are recorded when customers are billed, rather than when payment is received, and expenses when they are incurred, rather than when they are paid.

Amortization: The writedown of assets over a period of time to recognize their diminishing value as they are used.

Arm's length parties: Parties that are not related to each other and have no other connection that may cause them to treat each other more favourably.

Assets: Things that a business owns including: cash, accounts receivable, inventory, equipment, land, and buildings.

Asset-based method: A method of valuing a business based on its assets and liabilities.

Balance sheet: A statement of a business's assets and liabilities as of a specific date.

Book value: The cost of an asset less depreciation or amortization.

Business evaluation: An analysis of the merits of a business, which may include determining its dollar value.

Business valuation: The result, in dollars, of valuing a business.

Capitalized cash flow: Expected cash flow times a multiple.
Cash flow: The change in cash from one period to another, often a year.
Cash flow method: A method of valuing a business based on its cash flow.
Controlling interest: The shareholder interest that holds enough voting shares to outvote the other shareholders.
Current assets: Cash, accounts receivable, inventory and any other assets that, in the normal course of business, will be converted into cash within a year.
Current liabilities: Accounts payable and other amounts owing that are likely to be settled within a year.
CBV: Chartered Business Valuator
CPA: Chartered Professional Accountant
CRA: Canada Revenue Agency
Depreciation: The writedown of assets over a period of time to recognize their diminishing value as they are used.
Discounted cash flow method: A method of valuing a business based on the cash flow for each future year, for a specific number of years, discounted to their present values.
Discount rate: Rate of return used to discount cash flows to their present value.
Due diligence: The process of learning about a business.
Earnings: The net income or profit of a business.
EBITDA: Earnings before interest, income taxes, depreciation and amortization.
Enterprise value: The value of a business before deducting outstanding debt.
Expected cash flow: A reasonable assumption of how much cash can be generated based on the resources currently in place.
Fair market value: The highest price available in an unrestricted market between informed and prudent parties, acting at arm's length, and under no compulsion to act, expressed in terms of cash.

Generally Accepted Accounting Principles (GAAP): A common set of accounting principles, standards and procedures that companies may follow when they prepare their financial statements.

GIC: Guaranteed investment certificate, an investment paying a stated rate of interest.

Going concern: A business that will continue to operate and has the resources to do so.

Goodwill: The component of a business's value in excess of its net assets.

Gross profit: A business's total revenue and/or sales minus the cost of its goods sold.

Hypothetical or imaginary sale: An assumed sale, even though an actual sale may not occur.

Income statement: A statement of a business's sales, revenue and expenses for a specified period.

Intangible assets: Assets that are not physical in nature.

Liabilities: The amounts that a business owes to others including: accounts payable, bank loans and other debt.

Liquidation value: Value of an asset when it must be sold quickly.

Liquidity: The degree to which an asset or security can be readily bought or sold.

Market method: A method of valuing a business based on how much a comparable business sold for.

Minority discount: A discount applied to the pro-rata value of a minority interest to reflect its lack of control.

Minority interest: A shareholding in a company that is not the controlling interest.

MLS: The Multiple Listing Service for real estate.

Multiple: A number by which expected cash flow is multiplied by to arrive at a value for the business, and the inverse of a rate of return.

Net assets: Assets at their current values less selling costs and liabilities.

Net income: Sales and/or revenues less expenses.

Net proceeds: The value of the business less the outstanding debt.
Non-cash items: Income or expenses that arise from accounting entries rather than actual cash transactions including: depreciation, amortization, gains and losses on the sale or disposal of assets.
Open market transaction: A transaction between arm's length parties.
Owner's equity: Net assets.
Present value: The current worth of a future sum of money or stream of cash flows given a specified discount rate.
Proprietorship: A business that is not incorporated as a company.
Rate of return (ROR): The annual income from an investment expressed as a percentage.
Redundant assets: Assets that are not essential to a business's operations.
Rule of thumb: An easily applied procedure to estimate value.
Special purchaser: Buyers who may be able to realize benefits that others cannot.
Statement of business or professional activities: A statement similar to an income statement prepared by proprietorships or partnerships.
Value of a business: How much a business is worth in dollars.
Valuing a business: The process of arriving at a dollar value for a business.
Working capital: Current assets minus current liabilities; the funds available to a business in the short term.

Acknowledgments

In 2010 the Canadian Institute of Chartered Business Valuators launched the Ian R. Campbell research initiative and encouraged Canadian academics, students, and valuation practitioners to submit research proposals, with one to be chosen each year for an award and publication. I was delighted that my topic, *IFRS—Are We in for a Market Shock?* was selected that first year. Not only was it an honour to be published in the institute's Journal of Business Valuation, the award was instrumental in starting me down the writing path.

A few years later Harold Hutton, a former colleague and fellow Chartered Business Valuator, suggested that I write a book to help business owners understand valuation. Thanks, Harold, for seeing the need for a book such as this, and encouraging me to write it.

I'd also like to thank Barry Collins, Johan Dooyeweerd, Brock Ewing-Chow, Brian French, Bob Heilker, Harold Hutton, Adam Hyde, Emil Kitka, and Mitchell Ornstein for sharing your experiences. My stories and characters wouldn't be real without you.

To my family, friends, and others who were willing to read the early drafts: Johan Dooyeweerd, Cathy Hayes, Niko Hill, Barbara Ingram, Elizabeth MacRae, Ian McCarthy, Darryl Otteson, Karen Schultz, and Karen Stanley, your feedback, tips, encouragement and catching those missing commas, were invaluable.

As this is my first book, I had not had the opportunity before of working closely with an editor. The undertaking proved to be an absolute pleasure, a great learning experience and an invaluable second pair of eyes. For anyone thinking of self-publishing, hiring an editor is essential. Thank-you, Susan Chilton, for gracefully guiding me through the editing process from start to finish. Susan polished the wording a hundredfold without changing my voice, and offered advice not only on editing but all aspects of publishing. My other editor, Bernard Simon, also a master wordsmith, was instrumental in improving the flow of the manuscript to make it effective and engaging.

A book is so much more than the words. Thank you to, Toni Serofin, the designer who took my manuscript and transformed it into a book. The cover looks great! As for the book interior, I never knew how complicated that could be, especially when there are tables and charts, and an author who can't stop making one more change. Thank you, Toni, not only for your skillful and creative design but your patience as well.

– Liisa Atva